100 PLANTS
—for—
POTS &
Containers

100 PLANTS
for
POTS &
Containers

General Editor: Mary Moody

CRESCENT BOOKS

NEW YORK • AVENEL

Contributing writers: Mary Moody, Stephanie Watson

Published by Lansdowne Publishing Pty Ltd
Level 5, 70 George Street, Sydney NSW 2000, Australia

This 1995 edition published by Crescent Books,
distributed by Random House Value Publishing, Inc.,
40 Engelhard Avenue, Avenel, New Jersey 07001

Random House
New York • Toronto • London • Sydney • Auckland

First published 1994

© Copyright: Lansdowne Publishing Pty Ltd 1994
© Copyright design : Lansdowne Publishing Pty Ltd 1994

Managing Director: Jane Curry
Publishing Manager: Deborah Nixon
Production Manager: Sally Stokes
Project Coordinator: Kate Oliver
Copy Editor: Glenda Downing
Horticultural Advisor: Liz Ball
Design Concept: Catherine Martin
Typesetter: Veronica Hilton
Formatted in Galliard on Quark Xpress
Printed in Singapore by Kyodo Printing Co (S'pore) Pte Ltd

ISBN 0-517-12125-5

A CIP catalog record for this book is available from the Library of Congress.

KEY TO SYMBOLS

○	prefers full sun
◐	prefers partial shade
●	prefers shade
pH̬	acid soil
ṗH	alkaline soil
❖	half-hardy – temperatures down to 0°C
❖❖	hardy – temperatures down to -5°C
❖❖❖	fully hardy – temperatures down to -15°C

Contents

Introduction

✿ **POTS FOR PRACTICAL PURPOSES** There are many excellent reasons why gardeners choose to grow plants in containers rather than directly in the ground. For renters and apartment dwellers, container-grown plants are often the only garden that is practical. Most potted plants, with the exception of large ornamental trees and climbers, can be easily moved from one location to another, creating a 'garden-to-go' for those on the move.

In cool to cold climates, many plants can be grown in containers that otherwise would not be suited to this particular climate. Tender species can be brought outside in spring, when the danger of frost has passed, and placed in a warm, sheltered position until autumn, when they will need to be brought under cover once again. This tradition is practised routinely in Italy, where groves of orange and lemon trees are dragged into the sun every summer.

In some regions, the soil prohibits the cultivation of certain plants. Where the existing soil is alkaline, delightful plants such as camellias, azaleas, and rhododendrons will never thrive. In a container, however, they can be treated to an acid potting mixture that will entirely suit their particular pH requirements. Likewise, poor soil drainage is a problem in some regions, or even in certain areas of the garden. Where heavy clay soil is a problem, it can be overcome either by creating raised beds, above ground level, or creating a landscape in containers that will provide the ideal growing conditions.

Many keen gardeners grow a variety of plants in containers to provide a splash of colour all year round. These plants can be raised in a warm, sheltered situation, even in a greenhouse or glasshouse, then brought to a prominent position when in full bloom. They can be clustered together near the main entrance to the house or garden to give a warm, welcoming effect.

There are many trailing and cascading plants that are displayed to their best effect when growing in a hanging basket. The elevated container, if well watered and fed, should provide a perfect growing environment, and one that will allow the flowering stems or foliage to hang over the edges of the basket.

Finally, growing plants in containers can be done simply for sheer effect. It is a great way to make a special feature of a particular favourite plant, or to create a miniature garden on a balcony, patio, or verandah that would otherwise be bare of foliage and flowers. Smaller plants, such as miniature roses, can be overwhelmed or 'lost' in large garden beds or borders, but really come into their own when well displayed in an attractive container.

✿ **CHOOSING THE BEST CONTAINER** It is important to select a container that not only looks good, but works well for the particular plants being used. Some plants require perfect drainage and, therefore, a natural terracotta container is probably the most effective, because it is light and porous and provides the correct growing conditions. Terracotta tends to dry out very quickly, however, especially if positioned in direct sunlight, or where drying winds can cause evaporation. So take care to ensure the potting soil does not dry out completely when using terracotta by watering daily, or even more frequently in hot, dry weather. Also, terracotta tends to be brittle and can break easily if knocked or bumped when being moved around.

Plastic containers have improved in looks over the past few years. Plastic is lightweight and durable, making it easy to move the plants around for effect or for climate control. Take care to place plenty of drainage rubble in the base of the container, however, as plants potted in plastic can become waterlogged, especially if sitting in plastic drip trays.

Concrete is a handsome material for containers, and is frequently used for large trees and shrubs. It is very heavy and hard to move around, so select a permanent position and ensure that the plant being used is comfortable with those particular requirements.

One of the most attractive finishes for plant containers is glazed ceramic. This is an ideal material for ornamental display, because it has the beauty of terracotta without the porous qualities. Styles vary considerably, according to the potter, and can be chosen to complement the colours and style of the house.

Timber, in the form of recycled wine barrels, is sometimes used as a plant container. Eventually it will rot, even if chemically treated, so be prepared to repot after a few years.

The size and shape of the container is also important. For example, ferns prefer slightly crowded root conditions, so a container should be chosen that is only slightly larger than the root mass. Most vigorous-growing plants need a container that will allow some space for expansion, especially some of the larger trees and shrubs. Never attempt to cram a plant into a container that is too small. Not only will it appear out of balance (that is, the top of the plant will be out of proportion with the base), but it will soon fail to thrive.

✿ **PERFECT POTTING MIXTURES** Container-grown plants will not thrive if potted into soil from the garden. Ordinary garden soil will quickly become compacted, preventing air and moisture from reaching the plant roots. The best solution is to invest in a good-quality commercial potting mixture that contains all the essential nutrients each plant will require for the first six months of growth, plus the correct texture for successful cultivation. A good potting mixture must be light enough to allow free air circulation and water drainage, but also contain enough organic matter to retain a certain amount of soil moisture so that the nutrients can reach the root system of the plant. Poor-quality potting mixes are usually too light and dry out very quickly, and contain little or no nutrients to keep plants growing.

It is possible to make your own rich potting mixture using the following ingredients:

2 parts loam (good garden soil)
1 part leaf litter or peat (to aid moisture retention)
1 part coarse sand (to aid free drainage)
2 handfuls of blood and bone per bucket of potting mixture
(to provide basic nutrients)

This mixture can be varied considerably to suit the individual requirements of plants. For example, ferns prefer a special slow-release fertilizer formulated specifically for their growth requirements, which can be used instead of the blood and bone. Vigorous and fast-growing plants that are heavy feeders may require the addition of extra fertilizer or some well-rotted animal manure or good garden compost. Leafy vegetables that demand plenty of high-nitrogen fertilizer will need extra well-rotted poultry manure to get them off to a good start.

✿ **POTTING AND REPOTTING** Always clean containers thoroughly before introducing a new plant to prevent the possibility of soil-borne diseases being transferred from one plant to another. A scrub with hot, soapy water should be sufficient, making sure the container is well rinsed afterwards. The soil around the plant should be lightly moist — never dry and never waterlogged — prior to potting. The potting soil should also be damp (again, not wet but not dry). Line the base of the container with some gravel or broken terracotta pot, making sure that the drainage holes are not clogged up. Take care when removing the plant from its original container by cradling the root in the palm of your hand and lifting it out intact. If it is seriously root bound it may be necessary to cut the pot with sharp secateurs, or to run a sharp knife around the inside of the pot to loosen it. Gently tease the roots to loosen them if they have formed a tight ball, as this will help them to adjust to the new container. Repot immediately, surrounding the root mass with the fresh potting mixture. Press down firmly, but not too hard, making sure that the plant is not buried below the original surface level. Water thoroughly and place the container in a shady, sheltered position for at least two weeks, giving it time to adjust before putting it into direct sunlight.

✿ HOW TO USE THIS BOOK

This book has been designed as a simple guide to successfully cultivating all the plants listed. The soil pH level has been specified only when it needs to be either acid or alkaline, according to the particular requirements of the plant. All other plants can be easily grown in soil in the neutral range (that is, pH 7.0). Refer to the key to symbols on page 4.

A plant's preference for sun, partial shade or full shade, and its hardiness rating are also indicated by symbols. The hardiness symbols indicate each individual plant's ability to withstand winter temperatures and frost and apply if the potted plant is positioned outdoors year round. No symbols have been given for annuals, which are only grown from spring to autumn in cool and cold climates, and therefore are not expected to survive winter.

The mature height of plants, indicated under 'Description', may vary from one climate to another, sometimes only reaching the maximum size in the country in which it is a native species.

Where advice has been given on pests and disease infestations, this is meant as a guide to a certain plant's susceptibility to a particular problem. Treatment of that problem will vary from one country to another.

Abies balsamea 'Hudsonia'
Dwarf balsam fir ◑ pH ❖❖❖

✿ **DESCRIPTION** A handsome dwarf conifer that is ideally suited to
container cultivation in a wide variety of climates. Growing to 3 feet (1 m)
in height, with a similar spread, it has attractive smooth, greyish bark and
grey-green needle-like foliage that is arranged in a spiral fashion. It has
small, resinous cones that are soft violet when young. Because of its outline,
which is rather flat and spreading, it will require a container with a rounded,
broad shape. ✿ **PLANTING** Choose a solid container and line the base
with a layer of small rocks or broken terracotta to prevent the drainage hole
from becoming clogged. Use a moderately rich, well-drained potting
mixture that has had a handful of slow-release all-purpose fertilizer added.
✿ **FLOWERING** Bears cones in spring. ✿ **CULTIVATION** Water
weekly, and repot every three or four years, depending on how much the
tree has grown and the size of the container. Aphids are sometimes
attracted to the new growth, and also keep a watch for bark beetles.
✿ **PROPAGATION** From seed sown in autumn in cool to cold climates
or, in temperate climates, from stratified seed that has been mixed with sand
and chilled for two months in the refrigerator prior to planting out.

Acer palmatum 'Dissectum Atropurpureum'
Japanese maple ◐ ❖❖❖

❀ **DESCRIPTION** One of the most outstanding of all the maples, this delightful small-growing tree looks wonderful in a container as a feature plant on a balcony or verandah, or in a sheltered position in the garden. Reaching 15 feet (4.5 m) in height after many years of growth, specimens kept in a container are generally smaller. The Japanese maple is a bushy, deciduous tree with a rounded top and arching branches of deeply divided red-bronze or purple foliage that turns a richer red, orange, or yellow during autumn. It also has small, red-purple flowers that blend in with the foliage. ❀ **PLANTING** Look for a container that will highlight rather than compete with the beauty of the foliage. Plant into a well-drained but humus-rich potting mixture, and water in well. Position where strong winds cannot damage the sensitive foliage, and mulch the surface of the potting mixture with organic matter. ❀ **FLOWERING** The rather insignificant flowers appear in spring. ❀ **CULTIVATION** Only transplant into a larger container every five years, as growth is slow. Sprinkle all-purpose fertilizer on the soil surface in spring, and water weekly, more frequently if weather is hot and dry. ❀ **PROPAGATION** From seed sown either when ripe or in autumn.

Acmena smithii (syn. *Eugenia smithii*)
Lili-pili tree ○ ◐ ❖

❖ **DESCRIPTION** An interesting evergreen tree that can be grown
in cooler regions if taken under cover during winter. Growing to 18 feet
(5.4 m) in height, it will remain smaller and more compact if cultivated
in a container. It is a very decorative plant, with large, glossy dark green
leaves. The variety 'Elizabeth Isaac' has leaves with silvery-cream markings.
The foliage, when it first appears, is a pretty, soft pink colour. It also has small
fluffy white flowers, borne in terminal clusters, followed by edible pink or
purple berries in winter. It is a useful balcony screening plant in coastal areas,
being resistant to salt spray. ❖ **PLANTING** Choose a sunny or semi-shaded
position, and plant into quite rich and well-drained potting mixture in
which some all-purpose fertilizer has been incorporated. Water well, and
keep in the shade for the first few weeks. ❖ **FLOWERING** The flowers
appear in summer, followed by the fruits. ❖ **CULTIVATION** This plant
will require plenty of watering when grown in a container, especially during
summer. Mulch the surface of the potting soil, and feed annually with a
general purpose fertilizer in spring. It is usually quite pest and disease resistant.
❖ **PROPAGATION** From ripe seed, sown in winter.

Buxus sempervirens

BOX ○ ◑ ❖❖❖

❁ **OTHER NAME** Common box ❁ **DESCRIPTION** A useful and
hardy evergreen shrub that is excellent for growing in a container, either as
a feature plant or as a hedge with potted plants arranged in a row. Native to
southern Europe, the box can grow to a height of 18 feet (5.4 m) unless
trimmed, and is very long-lived, which makes it ideal as a permanent feature
in the formal garden. The deep green foliage is small, oblong, and glossy
and there are several worthwhile varieties including 'Albo-marginata',
which has green and white margined leaves, and 'Suffruticosa', which is a
dwarf form with mid-green leaves, and is frequently used as an edging
plant. The smaller forms are often used for topiary. The flowers are
insignificant. ❁ **PLANTING** Box will thrive in a well-drained, moderately
rich potting mixture that has been enriched with peat to help it retain
moisture during summer. Mulch the soil surface with compost, and water
after transplanting. ❁ **FLOWERING** The flowers are small and
insignificant. ❁ **CULTIVATION** Trim into shape several times a year.
Encourage vigorous new growth by cutting back stems to 1 foot (30 cm) or
less in late spring. ❁ **PROPAGATION** Semi-ripe cuttings can be taken in
summer.

Chamaecyparis lawsoniana 'Ellwood's Gold'

Lawson cypress ○ ❖❖❖

✿ **DESCRIPTION** A delightful small-growing conifer that makes a perfect plant for a container when positioned in a sunny place where the beauty of the foliage can be truly appreciated. It is an upright, evergreen plant that can reach 10 feet (3 m) when grown in the ground, and slightly smaller when cultivated in a pot. It has a slender, columnar form. This variety has pale, silver-green foliage overlaid with gold, which appears brighter in winter. The small cones vary in colour between male and female plants.

✿ **PLANTING** Select a container that will not outshine the foliage of the plant, and use a fairly rich potting soil, making sure that the drainage holes at the base of the container are not clogged. Keep the young plant in the shade for a few weeks until it has acclimatized, then position in full sun.

✿ **FLOWERING** Cones appear in spring. ✿ **CULTIVATION** Lawson cypress is a very slow-growing plant that will only need repotting every five or six years. Water routinely, especially in summer, and use a mild, slow-release all-purpose fertilizer, applied in early spring.

✿ **PROPAGATION** From cuttings taken in autumn, or grafts onto Lawson cypress understock.

Ficus benjamina
Weeping fig ○ ◑ ❖

✿ **OTHER NAMES** Benjamin fig, Java fig

✿ **DESCRIPTION** One of the most useful trees for growing in a container, this handsome specimen can be grown outdoors in warm areas, and inside where winters are cold. Although in its native environment of Indonesia it can grow to 50 feet (15 m), it will not reach anywhere near this size when cultivated in a pot. It has spreading, drooping branches and a good covering of shiny, mid-green oval leaves that have a leathery texture. There is a variegated form, 'Variegata', which has a bushy, weeping habit and lustrous green and white variegated foliage. The flowers are insignificant, and the small red fruits are not edible. ✿ **PLANTING** Choose a container that is larger than the root mass of the fig, and surround it with plenty of good-quality, lightly moist potting mixture. Mulch the surface of the potting mix if the container is in direct sun. ✿ **FLOWERING** The flowers and fruits are insignificant. ✿ **CULTIVATION** If growing indoors position in a place that receives plenty of light, but not direct sunlight. Water only when the potting mixture begins to dry out, especially during winter when overwatering will cause the foliage to drop. Red spider mite can be a problem. ✿ **PROPAGATION** Either by seed sown in spring, or layering in summer.

Juniperus communis 'Compressa'

Juniper ○ ◐ ● ❖❖❖

✿ **OTHER NAME** Dwarf juniper ✿ **DESCRIPTION** A hardy and easy-to-grow conifer that looks very pretty when grown in a container as a feature plant, or at the back of a mixed grouping of pots. Growing to only 2 feet (60 cm) in height, it forms an upright column with curved sides, making a strong outline. The foliage is fine, aromatic, and needle-like in shape, in the mid to yellow-green colour range, sometimes turning slightly brown in winter. It produces fleshy, greenish berries that turn blue and eventually black with age. This conifer is sometimes planted in groups to form a miniature hedge. ✿ **PLANTING** Transplant into a solid container using a good-quality potting mixture that is capable of holding moisture, especially during summer. ✿ **FLOWERING** The berries are held on the plant for several years. ✿ **CULTIVATION** Avoid overwatering in winter, but ensure that the potting mixture does not become completely dry, especially during summer. If positioned in the sun, mulch the surface with some well-rotted compost. Apply a small amount of slow-release, all-purpose fertilizer once a year in spring, and repot into a larger container if necessary. ✿ **PROPAGATION** The seeds are very slow to germinate, even when stratified to break the dormancy (mixed with sand and stored in the refrigerator for several months). Hardwood cuttings can be taken in autumn but, once again, they are sometimes difficult to strike.

Laurus nobilis

Sweet bay ○ ◑ ● ❖❖

✿ **OTHER NAME** Laurel ✿ **DESCRIPTION** This handsome tree is the one from which we get the aromatic bay leaves commonly used in cooking. When grown as a container plant it is frequently clipped as a standard, which looks most effective. In cooler climates it will need to be taken indoors over winter; however, otherwise it is quite robust and easy to cultivate. Growing to 30 feet (9 m) in the wild, it will not reach anywhere near this size in a pot. It is prized for its aromatic, leathery, and somewhat glossy dark green foliage. The pale yellow flowers are small and star-like, followed by green fruits that turn black as they mature. ✿ **PLANTING** The potting mixture should be quite rich and fertile with plenty of well-rotted compost added, as well as a slow-release, all-purpose fertilizer. Position the pot where it gets some shelter from strong winds and winter frosts. ✿ **FLOWERING** Small flowers appear in spring, followed by fruits. ✿ **CULTIVATION** Once established in the container it is quite an easy plant to care for, although it must be watered regularly in summer if conditions are hot. Trim back or shape during summer. ✿ **PROPAGATION** Either by seed sown in autumn, or from semi-ripe cuttings taken in summer.

Malus pumila

Apple ○ ❖❖❖

❀ **OTHER NAME** Common apple ❀ **DESCRIPTION** There are many varieties of the apple tree that can be grown successfully in a container, including the new columnar varieties which produce only a single, upright stem that bears both flowers and fruits. These are ideal for small containers for balcony gardens, but any of the domestic apple trees can be grown successfully in a large pot if pruned back hard to maintain a compact shape. The species *pumila* bears small crab apples, and the fully fruiting varieties can also be cultivated. Growing to 30 feet (9 m) when grown in the ground, they are prized for their glorious spring blossom, which are white suffused with pink, and their attractive, edible fruits. ❀ **PLANTING** Apples are quite heavy feeders and, as such, should be planted into a rich and well-drained potting soil that has had plenty of well-rotted compost and all-purpose fertilizer added. ❀ **FLOWERING** Blossom covers the tree in spring. ❀ **CULTIVATION** Do not allow the potting soil to dry out completely, especially in summer. Fertilize in early spring and again in late summer, then prune back hard in winter to maintain a good vase shape. ❀ **PROPAGATION** Apples are propagated by budding in late summer, or by grafting in winter.

Prunus persica

Peach ○ ❖❖❖

❀ **OTHER NAME** Ornamental peach ❀ **DESCRIPTION** There are many varieties of peach that can be grown successfully in a large container. They are valued for their wonderful spring blossom as well as their pleasant shape and foliage. Peaches are deciduous trees, growing to 14 feet (4.2 m) in height, with a short trunk and, vase-shaped upward branches. The foliage is lance-shaped and mid-green, turning a yellow-green in autumn. The blossom varies considerably according to the variety, including 'Double Crimson', which has large, double rose-red flowers; 'Double White', which has semi-double, pure-white blossom; and the dwarf 'Tricolour', which grows to 6 feet (1.8 m) with white flowers splashed with pink. There are several weeping forms, which also look attractive in a large pot.
❀ **PLANTING** To produce good results use a large container that is not porous, and make sure that the potting soil is rich with organic matter that will hold moisture in summer. ❀ **FLOWERING** Blossom appears in profusion in spring. ❀ **CULTIVATION** Water well in summer, especially when conditions are hot and dry. Use a slow-release, organic fertilizer in spring to boost growth, and again towards the end of summer.
❀ **PROPAGATION** By seed sown in autumn, or from hardwood cuttings taken in winter.

Washingtonia filifera
Californian fan palm ○ ❖❖❖

✿ **OTHER NAME** Desert fan palm ✿ **DESCRIPTION** Palms can be successfully grown in containers for many years, even in cooler climates where they must be brought indoors to a well-lit area during winter. They make ideal plants for outdoor entertaining areas, or near poolsides. Reaching to 60 feet (18 m) in height when planted in the ground, they will not reach anywhere near this size in a pot. They are a tall growing, slender plant with a greyish, textured trunk and a topnotch of grey-green leaves that are fringed with long, white fibres. The flowers are small and white, and appear in clusters. ✿ **PLANTING** The beauty of these palms is that they can withstand quite dry soil, and can be successfully cultivated in any moderately rich, well-drained potting mixture. Choose a sunny, open position and mulch the surface of the potting soil after planting. ✿ **FLOWERING** The small flowers appear in summer. ✿ **CULTIVATION** Once established they are quite a low-maintenance pot plant, and will only require a weekly watering in summer. Reduce watering in winter, and bring indoors if the climate is cold. ✿ **PROPAGATION** By seed sown in spring.

Catharanthus roseus (syn. *Vinca rosea*)
Madagascar periwinkle ○ ❖

❀ **DESCRIPTION** A most attractive, small evergreen shrub that is grown as an annual in cool climates because it cannot withstand frost. If necessary, however, it can be positioned in full sun during summer, then brought into a light, protected area during winter. Growing to 2 feet (60 cm), it has a spreading shape that can become untidy unless pruned. The foliage is dark green and oval, while the flowers are phlox-like and either rose-pink or white in colour, with a pink or red eye. ❀ **PLANTING** The potting mixture for this plant must be light and well drained, and the base of the container should be lined with gravel or pieces of broken terracotta to ensure the drainage holes are not blocked. Place in an open, sunny position. Terracotta is a good container because it is light and porous. ❀ **FLOWERING** Flowers over many months, from spring through to autumn. ❀ **CULTIVATION** Only water moderately, except during very hot weather, and reduce watering in winter as this plant resents waterlogged soil conditions. Long or straggly stems can be pruned back hard in early spring to encourage a more bushy growth. ❀ **PROPAGATION** By seed sown in spring, or from semi-ripe cuttings taken in summer.

Camellia japonica

Camellia ◐ pH ❖❖❖

✿ **DESCRIPTION** The highly-prized camellia is very easy to cultivate in a container if the correct soil conditions are provided. Plants vary considerably within the japonica group. In general, camellias are largish shrubs with a good covering of deep green, glossy foliage and a showy display of waxy flowers that can be single, semi-double, or double in a variety of colours, including white, pink, red, or variegated forms. ✿ **PLANTING** Camellias will thrive in moderately rich, moist, and slightly acid potting mixture in a semi-shaded situation. Afternoon sun is preferable to morning sun, especially for the pale flowered varieties, which will get scorched petals. Water well until established. ✿ **FLOWERING** Varies according to the variety, but generally from late winter to early summer. ✿ **CULTIVATION** Like all shallow-rooted plants, camellias like a good layer of leaf mulch to prevent the soil surface from drying out. Feed annually, when flower buds are forming or immediately after flowering, with a specially formulated camellia fertilizer. Aphids, thrips, and scale insects may cause a problem. Repot into a slightly larger container every four or five years, and prune if stems become leggy or lax. ✿ **PROPAGATION** From semi-ripe cuttings taken in summer, or from hardwood cuttings taken in winter.

Cotoneaster horizontalis
Rock spray ○ ◑ ❖❖❖

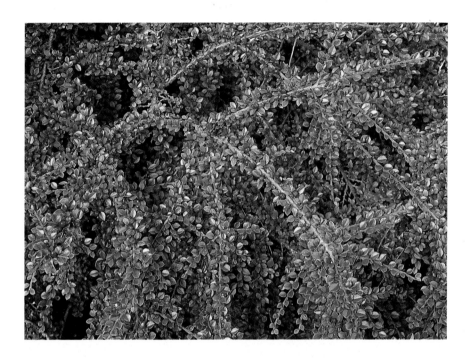

✿ **OTHER NAME** Wall spray ✿ **DESCRIPTION** A tough and easy-to-grow deciduous plant that is excellent in a large pot or tub, making a handsome display in full berry. This variety of cotoneaster grows to 3 feet (1 m) in height, with a spreading, horizontal branching habit that makes it useful for creating special features, such as low hedges or ground covers. From spring it is covered with masses of glossy, dark green foliage that changes to a soft red in late autumn. The pinkish-white flowers are small, followed by a wonderful display of bright red berries along the stems. The form 'Variegata' has foliage edged with white, and looks particularly attractive in a balcony garden. ✿ **PLANTING** This plant is useful because it can withstand quite dry soil conditions that cannot be tolerated by many other species. Choose a sunny or semi-shaded position, and make sure that the potting soil is well-drained, never waterlogged. ✿ **FLOWERING** The small flowers bloom in summer, followed by red berries in autumn. ✿ **CULTIVATION** Mulch around plants to prevent perennial weed growth and water routinely in hot and dry conditions. ✿ **PROPAGATION** Easy to propagate from semi-ripe cuttings taken in summer.

Daphne odora

Winter daphne ◖ pH ❖❖

✿ **DESCRIPTION** An evergreen shrub to 4 feet (1.25 m), winter daphne is grown for its distinctively fragrant flowers in winter and spring. It makes a pleasant plant for a container, which should be placed in a position where its perfume can easily be appreciated. The variety 'Alba' has pure-white flowers; var. 'Variegata' has attractive gold-edged leaves. Daphne tends to be short lived, dying off unexpectedly, or it can become leggy; so always have a few cuttings ready to replace the mature plant. ✿ **PLANTING** Plant into well-drained potting mixture. Add some well rotted leaf mould to the mix to create the correct pH balance. ✿ **FLOWERING** The clusters of pinkish buds opening to pink and white flowers are prominently displayed at the tips of the branches.
✿ **CULTIVATION** Water routinely in summer, and feed with a slow-release azalea-camellia fertilizer in early spring. These are surfaced-rooted plants so once established keep mulched to discourage weed growth and keep soil moist. Do not cultivate around the roots as they dislike being disturbed, and only repot in mid winter if necessary. ✿ **PROPAGATION** Cuttings may be taken from early to mid-summer when the new growth is semi-ripe.

Erica carnea (syn. *Erica herbacea*)

Heath ○ ◑ pH ❖❖❖

✿ **OTHER NAMES** Spring heath, Winter heath

✿ **DESCRIPTION** A pretty, spreading evergreen shrub that makes a lovely pot plant, especially when placed in groups with a variety of different flower colours. Growing to only 1 foot (30 cm) in height, it spreads pleasantly to 18 inches (45 cm) or more. The needle-like foliage is mid to dark green in colour, while the small, tubular or bell-shaped flowers are in various shades of pink, red, and white. There are many useful varieties, including 'Springwood Pink', which is slightly smaller with deep pink flowers; 'Eileen Porter', which is rather slow growing with deep red flowers; and 'Springwood White', which is an outstanding cultivar with large, showy white flowers. ✿ **PLANTING** Like all of the heaths, a neutral to slightly acid potting soil is advisable, and good drainage is essential. Incorporate plenty of well-rotted leaf litter into the planting medium, and mulch the soil surface to aid the retention of moisture. ✿ **FLOWERING** Flowers from late winter through to early spring. ✿ **CULTIVATION** Water routinely, especially in summer when the plants are in full growth, however, take care not to overwater in winter as heath dislikes wet roots. Prune lightly after flowering to maintain a bushy shape. ✿ **PROPAGATION** From seed sown in spring, or from cuttings or layering in summer.

Euphorbia pulcherrima
Poinsettia ○ ◑ ❖

❀ **DESCRIPTION** A popular, evergreen potted plant for indoor display during winter, often seen as a Christmas decoration in the northern hemisphere. Poinsettias are easy-to-grow, although they are very frost sensitive and will need to be brought inside from mid-autumn until mid-spring in cool to cold climates. Growing to 12 feet (3.6 m) in the ground, they will not reach this size when grown in containers if they are pruned hard after flowering. The tiny yellow flowers are insignificant, but are surrounded by bright red or deep pink bracts that create a wonderful display. Forms include 'Crema', which has yellowish bracts, and 'Plenissima', which has double red bracts. ❀ **PLANTING** Pot into a medium-size container in moderately rich, moist, but well-drained potting mixture. Potted plants from a nursery will probably require repotting after 12 months.
❀ **FLOWERING** Insignificant flowers with showy bracts during winter.
❀ **CULTIVATION** Water well, but do not allow the potting soil to become waterlogged. Prune back hard after flowering. Apply a slow-release fertilizer in spring. ❀ **PROPAGATION** From cuttings taken in summer, or by division in early spring.

Fuchsia hybrids
Fuchsia ◑ ❖❖

✿ **DESCRIPTION** This large group of plants contains some really delightful flowering varieties that are easy to grow in containers and look wonderful on a balcony or verandah. They are temperate climate plants, but are suitable for very cold and very hot climates where they can be moved to shelter when necessary and will need to be brought inside during winter in cooler climates. They can withstand temperatures down to 27°F (-5°C), but they resent very long, hot summers. Fuchsias are deciduous or semi-evergreen in habit, losing their foliage only in colder climates when under stress. Flowers and foliage vary considerably according to the variety, however all the flowers are tubular and pendulous, often with more than one petal colour. ✿ **PLANTING** Plant in a sheltered, semi-shaded situation in moderately rich potting mix that retains moisture but still has excellent drainage. ✿ **FLOWERING** The flowering period is extensive, from early summer through to late autumn. ✿ **CULTIVATION** Mulch the potting soil well with organic matter to provide slow-release nutrients. Water well, especially in summer, and stake those varieties where the weight of the flowers drags the stems down. ✿ **PROPAGATION** Very easily propagated with softwood cuttings taken at any time of the year.

Gardenia augusta (syn. *Gardenia jasminoides*)

Gardenia ○ ◑ pH ❖

✿ **DESCRIPTION** Although not hardy, gardenias make wonderful specimens in containers, which can be brought into a sheltered position during winter. Native to China, they are prized for their masses of glossy, dark green foliage and their fragrant flowers that can be enjoyed more if the container is positioned on a verandah or outdoor entertaining area. Growing to 4 feet (1.2 m) in the ground, gardenias can be maintained at a smaller size in the container with routine pruning. The leathery foliage is most attractive, and the waxy, single white flowers appear over many months. Varieties include 'Florida', which has very large double flowers, and 'Radicans', which is a slightly more compact form. ✿ **PLANTING** Gardenias must have a rich but well-drained potting mix that is in the neural to slightly acid pH range. Add plenty of well-rotted leaf litter, and mulch the soil surface to prevent it drying out in summer. ✿ **FLOWERING** Flowers over a long period from summer through to winter. ✿ **CULTIVATION** Water well in spring and summer when the plants are making growth, but take care not to overwater during the dormancy period. Prune back stems after flowering to prevent the shape of the shrub from becoming leggy. ✿ **PROPAGATION** From semi-ripe cuttings taken in summer.

Hibiscus syriacus

Rose mallow ○ pH ❖❖❖

✿ **OTHER NAMES** Shrub althea, Syrian rose

✿ **DESCRIPTION** One of the hardiest and easiest of the hibiscus group to cultivate, the rose mallow is valued for its beautiful, bell-shaped flowers that are in a wide range of colours. A native of China, it can be grown in a large container if pruned hard in early spring. Growing to 15 feet (45 m) in the ground, it is a deciduous, upright shrub with a good coverage of small, mid-green leaves and very showy flowers that range in colour from white through to purple, violet-red, and lavender. Some flowers have crimson centres and prominent veins. Useful cultivars include 'Mauve Queen', which has showy mauve flowers with red centres, 'Blue Bird', which is smaller growing with single, violet-blue flowers, and 'Diana', which is also a small shrub with showy, pure-white flowers. ✿ **PLANTING** Hibiscus prefer a slightly acid potting mix that is light and friable with good drainage. Incorporate some additional coarse river sand and well-rotted leaf litter to get the best results.

✿ **FLOWERING** Flowers appear in profusion from late spring right through summer. ✿ **CULTIVATION** Water routinely during the main growing periods of spring and summer, and feed with a slow-release fertilizer to encourage good flower production. In spring, prune back hard the previous year's growth. ✿ **PROPAGATION** Easy to propagate from hardwood cuttings taken in mid to late winter.

Hydrangea macrophylla

Garden hydrangea ○ ◑ ❖❖❖

✿ **DESCRIPTION** A popular, deciduous shrub with large pink, red, blue, or white blooms that usually grows to a height of 5 to 6 feet (1.5 to 1.8 m) and spreads from 6 to 8 feet (1.8 to 2.4 m). The flower colour varies according to the pH of the soil, with the exception of the white varieties. Neutral or alkaline soils produce pink or red hydrangea blooms, while acid soil produces the blues. Dome-shaped flower heads appear during summer and large, green, shiny leaves appear mid-spring. Hydrangeas make excellent shrubs for a container on a balcony or verandah when pruned well to maintain a bushy, rounded shape. ✿ **PLANTING** In cooler regions, hydrangeas will grow quite happily in full sun. In warmer districts, choose a protected and lightly shaded position. The potting mix should be rich, moist, and well drained. Plant at any time of year. ✿ **FLOWERING** Blooms appear from summer through to autumn. ✿ **CULTIVATION** Keep the plant well watered throughout summer and fertilize during spring. Hydrangeas produce flowers on two-year-old wood, so remove the spent blooms immediately to give the plant a chance to produce new, vigorous growth. ✿ **PROPAGATION** Easily propagated from softwood cuttings taken in late spring or early summer, or semi-hardwood cuttings from mid to late summer.

Lavandula angustifolia (syn. *Lavandula officinalis*)
Lavender ○ ❖❖❖

✿ **OTHER NAME** English lavender, True lavender

✿ **DESCRIPTION** One of the most popular of all fragrant evergreen perennial herbs, lavender can be used as a delightful container plant positioned near a patio or outdoor living area where the fragrance of the flowers can be easily enjoyed. Growing to 3 feet (1 m) in height, it has an open, irregular outline and upright stems covered with small, greyish furry leaves that age to mid-green in colour. The small flowers are held on slender, upright spikes, and are lavender-mauve and highly fragrant. Varieties include 'Alba', which has white flowers; 'Hidcote', which has deep purple flowers and silvery-grey foliage; and 'Munstead Dwarf', which has blue-purple flowers.

✿ **PLANTING** Plenty of sunshine and moderately rich, well-drained potting mix will provide the appropriate growing conditions for lavender. Line the base of the container with gravel or broken pieces of terracotta to ensure that the drainage holes do not become clogged. ✿ **FLOWERING** The flowers continue to bloom for several months, from spring through to autumn.

✿ **CULTIVATION** Mulch well to help retain soil moisture. Trim plants lightly in early spring to encourage more dense growth.

✿ **PROPAGATION** From semi-ripe cuttings taken in summer.

Osteospermum ecklonis
White veldt daisy ○ ❖

❀ **OTHER NAME** White African daisy

❀ **DESCRIPTION** Fast growing, and long-flowering are the main characteristics of these striking perennial plants. Osteospermums are perfect for that hot spot in the garden, in a container, or for cascading over the sides of a hanging basket. *Osteospermum ecklonis* grows to a height of 3 feet (90 cm) with an equal spread. The flowers are pure-white, daisy-shaped and have smart, navy blue centres. The leaves are narrow and oval in shape. ❀ **PLANTING** For best results, plant during spring or summer and choose a sunny position. The warmer the position, the longer the flowering period. The potting mixture should be moderately rich, moist and well-drained but this plant will survive impoverished conditions.

❀ **FLOWERING** Flowers appear from late winter through to spring in warmer regions, and from summer to autumn in cooler zones.

❀ **CULTIVATION** Once established, this daisy requires minimal attention. It tolerates drought although in a container it must be watered routinely, especially if conditions are hot and dry. Dress with pulverized manure during spring and trim back excess growth during autumn to maintain bushiness. ❀ **PROPAGATION** Take semi-hardwood cuttings inlate summer or sow seed during early spring.

Pieris japonica

Pieris ◑ ● pH ❖❖❖

✿ **OTHER NAME** Japanese andromeda ✿ **DESCRIPTION** This shrub is quite fussy about soil conditions, but once established it will thrive with very little maintenance. Pieris is a handsome evergreen shrub that can grow to 9 feet (2.7 m) with an upright shape and very attractive foliage. The leaves are lustrous and deep green, however, the new foliage growth is a brilliant bronze and makes a dramatic display following the flowers. The flowers appear as dense sprays covered with urn-shaped, creamy white blooms that have a waxy finish. There are many varieties, including 'Christmas Cheer', which has delicate pink flowers and 'Variegata', which has variegated leaves with white margins. ✿ **PLANTING** Choose a semi-shaded position in preference to full shade if the spring foliage display is valued. The soil must be well-drained and acidic, but capable of holding moisture well. The addition of peat at planting time will help create an ideal growing environment. ✿ **FLOWERING** Flowers appear in spring, followed by bronze foliage tip-growth. ✿ **CULTIVATION** In cold climates the young foliage tips can be killed by frost in spring, so they should be trimmed off or given some protection. Mulch well with rotted leaf mould, and water deeply in dry summer conditions. ✿ **PROPAGATION** From semi-ripe cuttings, or soft-tip cuttings, taken in summer.

Plumbago auriculata

Cape plumbago ○ ◐ ❖

❀ **DESCRIPTION** A fast-growing, woody-stemmed shrub with a lax,
open habit that can be grown in a large container if pruned back to restrict
its shape. A cultivar has also been developed that is ideal for a hanging basket,
with slender trailing stems. It is a warm climate shrub, native to South Africa,
that will need to be moved indoors or into a greenhouse during winter in
cool to cold climates. Growing to 10 feet (3 m) if not pruned, it has a semi-
climbing habit and sparse, pale green leaves. The flowers, however, are quite
appealing: borne in clusters, they are a distinctive, clear blue colour. The
variety 'Alba' has attractive white blooms. ❀ **PLANTING** Will grow easily
in any moderately rich and well-drained potting mixture that has some
additional well-rotted compost added. Mulch the potting mix surface after
planting. ❀ **FLOWERING** Flowers over long periods in late spring and
summer. ❀ **CULTIVATION** Do not allow the potting soil to dry out in
summer, and apply some all-purpose, slow-release fertilizer in early spring to
encourage good flower production. Prune back in early spring, tidying up
the previous year's growth. ❀ **PROPAGATION** From semi-ripe cuttings
taken in summer.

Punica granatum
Pomegranate ○ ❖❖

❀ **DESCRIPTION** A handsome, deciduous, rounded shrub that makes an excellent potted specimen in warmer climates. In cool to cold areas it will need to be brought into the shelter of a greenhouse during winter. A native of southern Europe and Asia, it can grow to 15 feet (4.5 m) in the open ground, but will remain much smaller when cultivated in a container. It has slender, mid-green leaves and large, showy, bright red, funnel-shaped flowers with crumpled petals. The yellow or orange fruits are edible, but will only ripen in warmer climates. The variety 'Nana', or dwarf pomegranate, is a dwarf form, only growing to 1 foot (30 cm) in height, which can also be cultivated successfully in a small container. ❀ **PLANTING** Choose a sunny but sheltered position, and use a potting mix that is light and well drained but still capable of holding moisture during summer. ❀ **FLOWERING** The flowers appear in summer, followed by the fruits. ❀ **CULTIVATION** Keep the pot well watered in summer, but do not allow it to become waterlogged. Reduce watering in winter. Use an all-purpose fertilizer in spring.

❀ **PROPAGATION** Either from semi-ripe cuttings taken in summer, or from seed sown in spring.

Rhododendron species

Azalea ○ ◐ pH ❖❖

❀ **DESCRIPTION** A large group of useful shrubs that make wonderful specimens for a pot or container in virtually any position in the garden. Azaleas can withstand quite cold winters, and in very cold climates they may be taken under cover during winter for protection. There are a tremendous number of different azalea varieties to choose from, including the deciduous Mollis azaleas with their cream, yellow, and orange flowers. The Indica azalea is a popular evergreen species, with flowers in the salmon, pink, red, and carmine colour range. The Ghent azaleas are more hardy, with very showy flowers that range from white to pink, yellow, coral, orange, and scarlet. ❀ **PLANTING** Azaleas must have potting soil that is well drained yet moisture retentive with an acid pH level. Incorporate some well-rotted leaf litter and a handful of specially formulated azalea food when potting. Mulch the soil surface with pine bark or a similar organic material.

❀ **FLOWERING** Flowers from spring to summer, depending on the variety. ❀ **CULTIVATION** Keep the potting soil lightly moist at all times, especially during hot weather in summer. Dead-head flowers when the blooms have finished. ❀ **PROPAGATION** Either by layering or semi-ripe cuttings taken in late summer.

Rhododendron species

Rhododendron ⟳ ❖❖❖

✿ **DESCRIPTION** A wonderful group of evergreen, cool climate shrubs that contains many smaller-growing varieties that make excellent plants for containers. Although some species grow to 40 feet (12 m), there are many that are 5 feet (1.5 m) or under which are ideal for the purpose. Rhododendrons are native to the eastern Himalayas and western China, and are valued for their attractive foliage, which is mid to dark green and sometimes variegated, and the large, showy flowers that are in a wide range of forms and colours.
✿ **PLANTING** Rhododendrons must have potting soil that is well drained yet moisture retentive with an acid pH level. Incorporate some well-rotted leaf litter and a handful of specially formulated azalea food when potting. Mulch the soil surface with pine bark or a similar organic material. Position in dappled light for the best results. ✿ **FLOWERING** Flowers from late spring onwards, depending on the variety. ✿ **CULTIVATION** Keep the potting soil lightly damp at all times, especially during hot weather in summer. Dead-head flowers when the blooms have finished. ✿ **PROPAGATION** Either by layering or semi-ripe cuttings taken in late summer.

Rosa 'Baby Darling'
Miniature rose ○ ❖❖❖

✿ **DESCRIPTION** A beautiful miniature rose that will make the most
wonderful display in a container positioned in full sun on a balcony or
verandah, or in a sheltered courtyard. Growing to 1 foot (30 cm) in height,
this variety was developed in the United States from a cross between 'Little
Darling' and 'Magic Wand'. It has a good covering of mid-green glossy foliage
and when grown correctly should produce an excellent display of double,
cupped, salmon-pink blooms over many months. The flowers are lightly
fragrant. ✿ **PLANTING** Roses must have a moderately rich and moist
potting soil, with some well-rotted compost added. Choose a medium-size
container and position in full sun. ✿ **FLOWERING** Flowers continuously
throughout summer. ✿ **CULTIVATION** Water routinely in spring and
summer but never allow the pot to remain waterlogged. Cut the flowers
regularly or dead-head spent blooms to encourage a longer flowering period,
and use a specially formulated rose food every six weeks from early spring to
boost flower production. In winter cut out any dead wood, and shorten
stems to create a more compact growth habit the following season.
✿ **PROPAGATION** From hardwood cuttings taken in autumn.

Rosa 'Benson & Hedges Special'
Miniature rose ○ ❖❖❖

❀ **DESCRIPTION** This delightful yellow rose is prized for the size of its blooms, which are larger and more showy than many miniatures. Developed in New Zealand, it is a cross between 'Darling Flame' and 'Mabella'. It grows to 1 foot (30 cm) in height, and has a particularly good, dense growth habit with masses of glossy, dark green leaves. The large, double flowers are rich yellow, and are carried on showy trusses. ❀ **PLANTING** Use a moderately rich potting soil that has been enriched with some extra compost or well-rotted manure, so that it holds moisture well during summer. Position in full sun, with some protection from strong prevailing winds.
❀ **FLOWERING** With care this rose should keep flowering for most of the summer. ❀ **CULTIVATION** Water routinely, especially when conditions are hot and dry. Use a specially formulated rose fertilizer at least twice a year — before and then during the flowering season — to encourage plenty of flowers. Dead-head spent blooms during summer, then cut out dead wood and prune back stems in winter. ❀ **PROPAGATION** From hardwood cuttings taken in autumn.

Rosa 'Magic Carousel'

Miniature rose   ○ ❖❖❖

✿ **OTHER NAME** Morrousel ✿ **DESCRIPTION** A useful small rose
that will look charming in a container placed on a sunny balcony or in a
courtyard. Growing to 15 inches (38 cm) in height, it has a handsome,
upright yet bushy shape and a good covering of clear green, glossy leaves.
The flowers of this rose are outstanding. They form a neat rosette shape
and are multipetalled, with cream centres and dark pink edges. They have
a delightful fragrance and make lovely cut flowers for indoor arrangements.
✿ **PLANTING** Use a good-quality potting mixture that contains
plenty of humus and peat to hold moisture during summer. Sprinkle
with some special rose food when the plant has become well established.
Mulch the surface to help prevent the potting mix from drying out.
✿ **FLOWERING** Flowers almost continuously during summer and
into early autumn. ✿ **CULTIVATION** Encourage prolific flowering
by frequent cutting of blooms or dead-heading spent flowers. Water
routinely, especially when the weather is hot and dry. Cut out dead
wood in winter, and also trim back stems to ensure compact growth
in the following season. ✿ **PROPAGATION** From hardwood cuttings
taken in autumn.

Santolina virens (syn. *S. rosmarinifolia*)
Green lavender cotton ○ ❖❖

✿ **DESCRIPTION** A charming, small evergreen shrub that makes a pleasant container plant because of its aromatic foliage and brightly coloured flowers. A native of the Mediterranean, it grows to 15 inches (38 cm) in height, with a bushy, spreading shape and finely cut, bright green fragrant foliage. The flowers are particularly attractive, held above the foliage on slender stems. They are vivid, yellow button-like heads. It is an easy plant to grow in a wide range of climates, however, it will need to be brought under cover in very cold regions, then put back out on display in the sunshine in spring. ✿ **PLANTING** This plant resents potting mix that is too rich, so stick to a standard formula and make sure that the drainage at the base of the container is quite free. Choose a sunny, open position.
✿ **FLOWERING** Flowers appear in spring. ✿ **CULTIVATION** Water routinely in summer, making sure that the potting mix is never waterlogged. Dead-head flowers after they droop, and cut back straggly stems in autumn. An early summer pruning will also encourage a more dense shape.
✿ **PROPAGATION** From semi-ripe cuttings taken in summer.

Spiraea cantoniensis
Chinese spiraea ○ ◐ ❖❖❖

✿ **OTHER NAMES** Reeves' spiraea ✿ **DESCRIPTION** *Spiraea cantoniensis* is a deciduous shrub known for its arching stems in reddish tones and its showy clusters of white flowers. The shrub itself is not outstanding for a large part of the year; however, the highly ornamental flowers are well worth the wait. It can grow to a height of 6 feet (1.8 m), although it will remain much smaller in a container if pruned back hard in early spring. The dark green, diamond-shaped leaves develop reddish tones during autumn. ✿ **PLANTING** Plant in a sunny or partly shaded position during spring or early summer into moderately rich, moist, and well-drained potting mixture. Incorporate generous quantities of compost and manure prior to planting and position the pot so there is sufficient room for spreading. It is a good background pot plant in a courtyard. ✿ **FLOWERING** Heavy flower clusters hang gracefully from the ends of the branches during late spring and early summer. ✿ **CULTIVATION** Spiraeas must be kept moist, so water well in spring and summer. Feed during early spring. The flowers of *Spiraea cantoniensis* only appear on the current season's growth, so prune during early spring before the new growth begins. ✿ **PROPAGATION** Cuttings may be taken at any time of the year.

Viburnum tinus
Laurustinus

✿ **DESCRIPTION** A most attractive evergreen shrub with a dense, bushy habit and a thick covering of oval, deep-green foliage. It can be grown as a container shrub if pruned back to prevent it from becoming too large. Growing to 10 feet (3 m) in the garden, it has flat heads of small white flowers which emerge from pinkish buds that cover the entire bush. The variety 'Lucidum' has larger and more showy flowers and a more open growth habit, but will not survive harsh growing conditions as easily as the species. Both will need to be taken into a greenhouse in cold climates.

✿ **PLANTING** While this viburnum can be grown in a semi-shaded position, it will produce a more prolific flower display when in full sun. The potting mix should be quite rich and well drained, and capable of holding moisture during hot weather. Add some extra peat or well-rotted compost, and mulch the surface of the pot to stop the mix from drying out in summer. ✿ **FLOWERING** Flowers from late winter through to mid-spring. ✿ **CULTIVATION** Keep well watered in spring and summer, then reduce watering when the cool weather sets in. Prune back in early spring to encourage a more dense shape. ✿ **PROPAGATION** From semi-ripe cuttings taken in autumn.

Clematis hybrids
Large flowered clematis ○ ◑ ❖❖❖

❀ **DESCRIPTION** Without doubt the most dramatic of all hardy
climbers, the large flowering hybrid clematis will make the most wonderful
display of flowers in early or late spring, depending on the cultivar. They
can be grown most successfully in a large container, and allowed to climb
over a trellis, archway, pergola, or against a wall. Clematis is a vigorous,
fast-growing twining climber that does not need to be trained if support is
provided. It has a good covering of oval, mid-green leaves and spectacular
flowers, some as large as a saucer, in a wide variety of colours from white
through pink to deep purple. Many of the flowers have dramatic markings,
which make them even more decorative. ❀ **PLANTING** Hybrid clematis
cannot tolerate its roots becoming warm, so position the container where
the root mass is completely shaded, even though the vine itself should be
climbing into the sun. Use a moderately rich and well-drained potting
mixture that has had some additional compost incorporated prior to planting.
❀ **FLOWERING** Flowers appear from early spring, depending on the
variety. ❀ **CULTIVATION** Water routinely, especially during warm
weather, and ensure that the container does not get any direct sunlight.
❀ **PROPAGATION** From softwood cuttings taken in summer.

Cobaea scandens
Cup and saucer vine ○ ◑ ❖

❀ **DESCRIPTION** A handsome, evergreen or deciduous woody-stemmed tendril climber that is tender and must be grown under glass or as an annual in cool or cold climates. It is very vigorous and makes a beautiful display against a sunny wall or trellis. Growing to 18 feet (5.4 m), it has masses of pointed, mid-green leaves and very large, showy flowers that are yellow-green when young, maturing to a rich purple. The flowers are a trumpet shape held above open bracts, hence the common name.

❀ **PLANTING** Use a large container and fill it with quite fertile but well-drained potting soil that has been enriched with additional compost and peat to help it hold moisture. Position it against some form of support such as a trellis or archway. ❀ **FLOWERING** Flowers for a long period during late spring and summer. ❀ **CULTIVATION** Water routinely, especially when the conditions are hot and dry. Mulch the surface of the pot to prevent the soil from drying out too quickly. Use a liquid organic fertilizer to boost flower production. ❀ **PROPAGATION** From seed sown in spring.

Hedera helix

Ivy ○ ◑ ● p̂H ❖❖❖

✿ **OTHER NAMES** English ivy, Common ivy ✿ **DESCRIPTION** Ivy
is a very fast growing and hardy climber that can be cultivated in a pot
positioned near any wall or trellis that needs to be covered quickly. The leaves
are normally five-lobed, shiny, and dark green, however, less-vigorous,
variegated types have been developed over recent years. The tough, woody
stems produce small aerial roots that cling firmly to any surface, growing up
to 34 feet (10.3 m) high with a spread of 17 feet (5.1 m). Once ivy has reached
the top of its support, it produces clusters of yellowish-green flowers. These
are soon followed by purple to black berries, which are poisonous. Ivy can
also be planted in window boxes, hanging baskets, or used in topiary work.
✿ **PLANTING** Plant during autumn or spring into an alkaline, moist,
fertile, and well-drained potting soil. Dark-leaved varieties will tolerate deep
shade, however, variegated types require a measure of sun. Ivy will need no
assistance to climb, however, ensure that the supports are strong enough to
take the weight of the mature plant. ✿ **FLOWERING** Insignificant
flowers appear during summer, followed by a mass of dark-coloured berries.
✿ **CULTIVATION** Prune and feed annually during spring, taking care if
you are susceptible to skin rashes. ✿ **PROPAGATION** By layering or
taking softwood cuttings during late summer.

Ipomoea alba
Moon flower ○ ❖

❀ **DESCRIPTION** A tender, fast-growing climber that can be grown as an annual in cool to cold climates. A native to tropical parts of the world, it is an excellent greenhouse plant in colder climates. It is a vigorous plant with soft stems that exude a milky sap when cut. It can be grown quite successfully in a medium to large container positioned against a sunny wall or archway that will provide support as it grows. The leaves are oval and mid-green, while the large and tubular flowers are white and quite fragrant. The flowers open out at dusk. ❀ **PLANTING** Use a moderately rich, moist, and well-drained potting soil that has had some additional organic matter added. Mulch the soil surface, and keep well watered until established. Provide some sort of support in the form of a trellis or pillar.
❀ **FLOWERING** Flowers appear in summer. ❀ **CULTIVATION** Water routinely in spring and summer, during the main period when growth is active. Reduce watering in autumn and winter. Mulch to keep weed growth from around the plant, and thin out dead wood during early spring.
❀ **PROPAGATION** Either by seed sown in spring, or from softwood cuttings taken during summer.

Jasminum polyanthum
Chinese jasmine ○ ◑ ❖❖

✿ **OTHER NAME** Pink jasmine ✿ **DESCRIPTION** A delightful woody-stemmed, evergreen twining climber that is wonderfully fragrant and can be grown in a large container against trellis or archways near the house, from where its fragrance can be easily enjoyed. It is quite a vigorous and easy-to-grow vine that will quickly cover a fence. The stems are well covered with dark green leaves, and for many weeks the entire vine is covered with clusters of small, white, fragrant flowers sometimes tinged with red on the outsides. The flowers are especially fragrant in the sun.
✿ **PLANTING** For best results, plant in moderately rich and well-drained potting mixture that has been enriched with organic matter. Water well until established, and provide support for the plant to twine and climb. In cold climates it is best planted in a greenhouse. ✿ **FLOWERING** Flowers for long periods from late spring well into summer. ✿ **CULTIVATION** Water routinely in summer, especially if conditions are hot and dry, and mulch to help retain soil moisture. Trimming may be necessary if the plant grows too large. ✿ **PROPAGATION** From semi-ripe cuttings taken in summer.

Lonicera japonica
Japanese honeysuckle ○ ◑ ❖❖❖

✿ **DESCRIPTION** Japanese honeysuckle grows at lightning pace, covering large walls and fences in no time at all. It can be planted in a large container to provide wall covering on a balcony or courtyard garden. It is evergreen in nature and has twining, woody stems, capable of climbing to a height of 15 feet (4.5 m) within a single growing season. The leaves are dark green, leathery to the touch, and form a dense cover. During late summer, masses of sweetly-scented, nectar-bearing blooms appear which are white in colour with a hint of purple. The flowers turn yellow as they mature and honeyeating birds find them very attractive. ✿ **PLANTING** Japanese honeysuckles should be planted during spring or autumn, into moderately rich, well-drained potting mixture. They may be grown in full sun or semi shade and require a strong form of support. ✿ **FLOWERING** Blooms appear from later summer through to autumn. ✿ **CULTIVATION** Keep moist throughout the growing season and feed with a complete fertiliser during spring and again in summer if the soil is impoverished. Regular pruning is essential to keep them under control. After flowering, remove old stems. ✿ **PROPAGATION** Japanese honeysuckle is easily propagated from layers or cuttings taken during late summer.

Mandevilla laxa
Chilean jasmine ◐ ❖

❁ **DESCRIPTION** A rather tender but charming semi-evergreen, woody-stemmed, twining vine that can be grown outdoors in warm climates and under glass or in a conservatory where the winters are cold. Growing to a height of 18 feet (5.4 m) it is a native of South America and, as such, needs plenty of warmth to grow successfully. It can be trained to cover a pillar, making a very pretty display when the flowers are blooming in summer. It is not a dense vine, but has an open, lax-growing habit and slender, heart-shaped leaves. The flowers are showy, quite large, and funnel-shaped. They are white to very pale pink in colour, with a pleasant fragrance.

❁ **PLANTING** Choose a semi-shaded position and use a medium to large container with moderately rich, moist, and well-drained potting soil. Position the container against a pillar or trellis to provide support as the vine grows. ❁ **FLOWERING** Flowers over several weeks in summer.

❁ **CULTIVATION** Water regularly during the main growth periods of spring and summer, then reduce water in autumn and winter. Thin out dead stems or congested growth in early spring. Red spider mite can be a problem during hot, dry weather. ❁ **PROPAGATION** From seed sown in early spring, or semi-ripe cuttings taken in summer.

Passiflora caerulea

Passionflower ○ ◑ ❖❖

✿ **OTHER NAMES** Common passionflower, Blue passionflower
✿ **DESCRIPTION** A most attractive vine from tropical and subtropical regions of the world, the passionflower can be grown successfully in a container. In cool to cold regions, choose a sheltered, sunny position or grow under glass. Growing to 18 feet (5.4 m), it can also be trimmed back hard, against a trellis inserted in the container, then brought into shelter if necessary. It is a wood-stemmed, tendril climber with masses of deep green, glossy leaves, and has very large and showy white or pink flowers with distinctive purple or blue-banded crowns and distinctive, deep red stamens. The flowers are followed by pale green fruits. ✿ **PLANTING** This vine will do best if planted into rich, moist, and well-drained potting soil that has some additional compost and peat added. Position in a semi-shaded area with a trellis or other support for the plant to grow on. ✿ **FLOWERING** Flowers from summer to autumn. ✿ **CULTIVATION** Water regularly in spring and summer, then reduce watering in autumn and winter. Thin out crowded growth in early spring, removing any dead wood or stems.
✿ **PROPAGATION** Either from seed planted in early spring, or from semi-ripe cuttings taken in summer.

Stephanotis floribunda
Madagascar stephanotis ◑ ❖

✿ **OTHER NAME** Wax flower ✿ **DESCRIPTION** A most attractive evergreen, woody-stemmed climbing vine that can be grown in a container on a sheltered balcony or courtyard in warm climates. In cooler climates it can be grown as an annual. It is quite a vigorous, fast-growing plant with masses of dark green, leathery leaves that have a glossy appearance. The flowers are carried in small clusters, and are the main feature of the plant. They are pure-white and starry in shape, with waxy petals and a distinctive fragrance. This vine can grow to 15 feet (4.5 m) or more, although it can also be trimmed back to a more manageable size in a container.

✿ **PLANTING** Use a medium-size container and moderately rich, moist, and well-drained potting soil that has been enriched with some well-rotted organic matter prior to planting. Water well until established.

✿ **FLOWERING** Flowers over a long period from spring to autumn.

✿ **CULTIVATION** Water regularly, especially during hot or dry weather. In autumn and winter, the watering can be reduced considerably.

✿ **PROPAGATION** Either from seed sown in spring, or from semi-ripe cuttings taken in summer.

Wisteria floribunda

Wisteria ○ ❖❖❖

❀ **OTHER NAME** Japanese wisteria ❀ **DESCRIPTION** One of the most highly prized of all climbing plants, the deciduous wisteria can be grown with great success in a container positioned in a sunny area on a balcony, verandah, or courtyard. It can be trained to climb up a supporting trellis or pillar, or clipped to be self-supporting in a container (initially, with the aid of a strong stake). Growing to 25 feet (7.6 m) when cultivated in a container, wisteria develops a very strong woody trunk from which twining tendrils emerge. The foliage is pale green and quite soft in texture, while the dramatic racemes of tiny flowers vary in colour according to the variety. 'Alba' has wonderful white flowers; 'Rosea' has rose-pink flowers with purple tips; and 'Violacea Plena' has double purple flowers in drooping racemes. ❀ **PLANTING** Use quite a large container filled with fertile, moist, and well-drained potting soil to which additional organic matter has been added. Make sure the drainage is adequate by lining the base of the container with stones or broken pieces of terracotta. Water well until established. ❀ **FLOWERING** Flowers from mid-spring to early summer, depending on the variety. ❀ **CULTIVATION** Water well in summer, especially when conditions are hot and dry. Help to train the tendrils in the direction that you want the plant to grow, and cut out any dead wood or untidy growth. Prune after flowering. ❀ **PROPAGATION** From seed sown in autumn or spring. Plants from seed may not flower as successfully as the grafted varieties from the nursery.

Armeria maritima
Thrift ○ ❖❖❖

❀ **OTHER NAMES** Sea pink, Armeria, Cliff rose ❀ **DESCRIPTION**
A hardy and useful clump-forming evergreen perennial that can be used
effectively as a potted plant, especially if two or more are established in one
container. Thrift forms an attractive clump of narrow, grass-like, mid-green
foliage, from which emerge stiff stems that carry delightful, circular flower
heads in various shades of pink and white. It grows to 6 inches (15 cm) in
height, and spreads slowly over several years. The variety 'Laucheana' has
outstanding, deep crimson flower heads. ❀ **PLANTING** Easy to grow in a
wide range of conditions if good drainage is present. Choose a sunny, open
position. Add some extra well-rotted compost to the potting mix to assist
with moisture retention. ❀ **FLOWERING** Flowers for many weeks
during late spring and summer. ❀ **CULTIVATION** Mulch around plants
to retard weed growth and to prevent the soil surface from drying out.
Water routinely, especially in hot, dry conditions. Remove spent flower
stems to encourage further flowering. ❀ **PROPAGATION** From semi-
ripe cuttings in summer, or from seed gathered in autumn.

Astilbe x *arendsii*
Hybrid astilbe ◑ ❖❖❖

❀ **DESCRIPTION** A handsome group of perennials valued for their attractive foliage and beautiful feathery spikes of white, pink, purple, or red flowers that appear over a long period in summer. Natives of Korea, China, and Japan, astilbes reach a height of 3 feet (1 m) or slightly more, forming a clump of foliage from which the strong, flowering stems emerge. In this group there are many excellent hybrids, including 'Fanal', which has bronze foliage and garnet-red flowers; 'Bressingham Beauty', which has rich pink flowers; and 'Granat', which has bronze-flushed foliage and crimson-pink flowers. ❀ **PLANTING** To grow successfully, astilbes must have quite rich, moist, and well-drained potting mixture. Add some well-rotted compost to the mix, and mulch after planting to prevent the potting mix from drying out during summer. Position the container in partial shade for the best results. ❀ **FLOWERING** The flowers appear for most of summer, looking attractive even when they dry out at the end of the season. ❀ **CULTIVATION** Water routinely during spring and summer, then reduce watering when the weather cools. Do not disturb unless the plant becomes pot bound and requires division. Add compost to the pot surface early each spring. ❀ **PROPAGATION** Either from seed sown in autumn, or by division of clumps in late winter.

Begonia rex

Begonia ◐ ❖

❀ **DESCRIPTION** These tender, rhizomatous plants make wonderful foliage plants for a sheltered and shady verandah or balcony. They can be grown under glass in cool to cold climates and brought outdoors in summer. Begonias, which vary in size according to the variety, are native to many tropical regions of the world and, as such, need quite warm growing conditions and shelter from cold winters. They are grown primarily for their outstanding foliage, which is large and often brightly coloured and patterned. The plant has creeping rhizomes that are also interesting and attractive, and are sometimes grown in a hanging basket where their beauty can be appreciated. ❀ **PLANTING** Begonias must have rich, well-drained potting soil and a container that is not too large, because they enjoy slightly cramped conditions. Choose a semi-shaded position and do no allow water to remain on the foliage, as this can cause botrytis. ❀ **FLOWERING** Flowers during summer. ❀ **CULTIVATION** Take care not to overwater these plants as they resent waterlogged conditions. Indeed, the potting soil should be allowed to virtually dry out between waterings. ❀ **PROPAGATION** Either by seed sown in spring, or from leaf cuttings or division of the rhizomes in early spring.

Bellis perennis

Daisy ○ ◑ ❖❖❖

✿ **OTHER NAME** English daisy ✿ **DESCRIPTION** A carpeting perennial or biennial plant that reaches a height of 4–6 inches (12–15 cm) and can withstand light frost and drought. There are single, semi-double, and double forms in shades of white, pink, and dark red, all with contrasting, yellow centres. The leaves are mid-green, oval in shape, and slightly hairy to the touch. They look very pretty when grown in a shallow container or trough which can be moved into a sheltered position during winter.
✿ **PLANTING** Grow in full sun to semi-shade in fertile, moist, and well-drained potting mixture. Plant during spring into a mixture that has been supplemented with well-rotted compost. Snails and weeds should also be kept at bay while the plant is established. ✿ **FLOWERING** The daisy flowers abundantly through late spring and summer.
✿ **CULTIVATION** Water well in dry spells, and mulch around plants to prevent the soil surface from drying out. ✿ **PROPAGATION** Sow seed outdoors in mild areas during late spring or summer, or sow in punnets under glass from early spring. Plants can also be readily divided in autumn, after flowering.

Campanula carpatica

Bellflower ◑ ❖❖❖

✿ **OTHER NAME** Carpathian bellflower ✿ **DESCRIPTION** This pretty, clump-forming perennial is often grown as a ground-covering plant, however, its shape makes it ideal for a container positioned in semi-shade on a balcony, verandah, or patio. Growing to 1 foot (30 cm) in height, it forms a pleasant mid-green mound of rounded or oval, toothed foliage that is mid-green in colour. The flowers are the main feature of the plant, being showy and bell-shaped in the violet-blue to white range. A compact, dwarf form, 'Blue Carpet', is also a good specimen for a pot, while the variety 'Bressingham White' has outstanding pure-white bellflowers. ✿ **PLANTING** To produce good results, use a broad, rather shallow container filled with quite rich, moist, and well-drained potting soil that has had additional compost added. Position in partial shade and protect from strong winds, especially during summer.
✿ **FLOWERING** Flowers for several weeks during summer.
✿ **CULTIVATION** Water routinely during spring and summer, then reduce watering when conditions become cooler. Only repot if the plant becomes potbound. ✿ **PROPAGATION** Either from seed sown in spring, division of clumps in autumn, or from softwood cuttings taken in summer.

Clivia miniata
Scarlet Kaffir-lily ◑ ❖

❀ **DESCRIPTION** A tender, evergreen rhizomatous perennial which makes a handsome potted houseplant that can be brought outdoors or onto a balcony during summer for an attractive display. Growing to 2 feet (60 cm) in height, it forms an attractive clump of strap-like, dark green leaves from which emerges sturdy stems with clusters of vivid orange or orange-red flowers, which are the main attraction of the plant. The variety 'Flava' has attractive yellow flowers. ❀ **PLANTING** This is a tough plant that will grow very well in a large pot in any moderately rich and well-drained potting soil. Add some extra organic matter before planting and position out of direct sunlight. ❀ **FLOWERING** Spring is the main flowering period. ❀ **CULTIVATION** Water routinely in summer and autumn, but reduce watering in winter. This plant should remain quite happily in the same container for about five years, when it can be divided and repotted in late spring, after flowering has finished. ❀ **PROPAGATION** Either by seed sown in spring, or by the division of clumps after flowering.

Cerastium tomentosum

Snow-in-summer ○ ❖❖❖

❁ **DESCRIPTION** This ground-covering plant is ideal for a pot or hanging basket, quickly spreading and cascading over the sides. It is a hardy, evergreen perennial that forms a dense carpet 3–6 inches (7.5–15 cm) high with a spread of 2–4 feet (60–120 cm). The white flowers are star-shaped and rest peacefully on small, silver-grey leaves. When in full flower, they cover the entire plant like a blanket of snow, hence the common name. ❁ **PLANTING** New plants or divisions are best planted during spring, at 1–2 feet (30–60 cm) intervals. Use a moderately rich, moist and well drained potting mixture that has been enriched with additional organic matter. ❁ **FLOWERING** A mass of flowers appear from late spring through to summer. ❁ **CULTIVATION** Cerastiums should be kept moist during the hot summer months and fed in spring with a complete fertilizer to encourage new growth. Pruning is not required, except to remove the dead flower heads at the end of summer. Hedge shears can be used for this purpose. ❁ **PROPAGATION** Easily started by seed, or from divisions taken during early spring or autumn.

Chrysanthemum frutescens (syn. *Argyranthemum frutescens*)
Marguerite ○ ❖

❀ **OTHER NAMES** Marguerite daisy, Paris daisy ❀ **DESCRIPTION**
Marguerite is a bushy, evergreen perennial plant, with a delightfully long
flowering period, which makes an attractive potted plant that can be grown
under cover or indoors where the climate is cold. The yellow-centred
flowers may be single or double and a variety of colours are available, from
pure white to yellow, and through to pink. The blooms are excellent as cut
flowers and are widely cultivated for this purpose. Under normal conditions,
the plant grows 2–3 feet (60–90 cm) high with an equal spread, and has a
neat, rounded appearance. The leaves are soft, light green, and deeply
divided and compliment the daisy-shaped flowers. ❀ **PLANTING** Plant
from spring through to autumn into fertile, moist, and well-drained potting
mix. Incorporate liberal amounts of compost into the mix prior to planting.
❀ **FLOWERING** Flowers may appear from winter through to autumn
but are most profuse during spring and summer. ❀ **CULTIVATION**
Marguerite daisies should be watered frequently throughout the growing
season especially if conditions are hot and dry. A dressing of complete
fertilizer during spring will reward you with a long flowering period.
Dead-head spent blooms regularly and trim to shape during early spring.
❀ **PROPAGATION** By seed or cuttings taken in spring.

Dianthus deltoides
Maiden pink ○ p̂H ❖❖❖

♣ **DESCRIPTION** A delightful evergreen, low-growing tufted perennial
that looks most attractive growing in a container on a sunny balcony or
verandah. A native of western Europe to eastern Asia, it grows to 15 inches
(38 cm) in height, forming a dense mat of tiny, lance-shaped leaves. The
flowers are small and have five petals, and are either cerise, white, or pink.
They are held above the foliage on slender stems. There are several outstanding
varieties, including 'Brilliant', which has bright red flowers, and 'Flashing
Light', which has blooms of rich cerise. ♣ **PLANTING** Pinks prefer a light
and well-drained potting mix that has a neutral to acid pH level. Choose a
sunny, open position and line the base of the container with gravel or pieces
of broken terracotta prior to planting. ♣ **FLOWERING** Flowers appear
from mid-spring to early summer. ♣ **CULTIVATION** Water routinely,
but ensure that the potting soil never becomes waterlogged. Watch for
red spider mite and aphids, which can be a problem. Pinks can remain
in the same container for quite a few years before transplanting.
♣ **PROPAGATION** From layering or cuttings taken in summer.

Erigeron karvinskianus
Mexican daisy ○ ❖

❀ **OTHER NAMES** Vittadinia, Fleabane ❀ **DESCRIPTION** Mexican daisy is a low, spreading, evergreen perennial that normally reaches a height of 1 foot (30 cm). It is a most attractive container plant, which can be brought into a greenhouse during winter in cool to cold climates. The stems have a fine, wiry appearance and produce small, narrow leaves. The daisy-shaped flowers have yellow centres and emerge pure white at first. Soon after, they turn pink and finally fade to a wine-red colour. The combined effect is most attractive. ❀ **PLANTING** Plant from spring through to autumn in an open, sunny position. The potting soil should be light, moist, and well drained for best results; with some extra organic matter added to help it retain moisture in summer. ❀ **FLOWERING** In mild regions, flowers appear throughout the year. Cold climate gardens will witness the blooms from late spring through summer. ❀ **CULTIVATION** Very little attention is necessary apart from regular watering throughout summer. A light feed with a slow-release fertilizer during early spring is also beneficial. Dead-head regularly to prevent self-seeding, otherwise allow them to run wild. In cold areas, cut the plants back hard during late autumn or move under shelter. ❀ **PROPAGATION** By seed or division of clumps in spring.

Helichrysum petiolare
Cudweed everlasting ○ ❖

✿ **DESCRIPTION** This charming, shrubby perennial is a native of South Africa, and will need to be placed in a greenhouse or under cover during winter. Growing to a height of 2 feet (60 cm), it will look most attractive in a container or hanging basket, because of its vine-like, weak stems that hang over the side and have a trailing effect. The foliage is lime-green with a woolly texture, while the flowers are particularly pretty, large, and showy in a soft shade of cream-yellow. ✿ **PLANTING** Choose a sunny, open position and a shallow pot or hanging basket filled with moderately rich, moist, and well-drained potting soil that has some additional compost added to help it retain moisture in summer. ✿ **FLOWERING** Flowers appear in summer. They can be cut while at their peak and dried for indoor arrangements. ✿ **CULTIVATION** Water routinely during spring and summer, then reduce watering as the weather cools in autumn. Feed annually with slow-release, all-purpose fertilizer and repot every three or four years if necessary. ✿ **PROPAGATION** From semi-ripe cuttings taken in summer.

Helleborus niger

Christmas rose ◑ ● ❖❖❖

❀ **DESCRIPTION** One of the most useful plants for late winter flowers, this charming perennial can be grown most successfully in a container positioned in a shady, sheltered area on a balcony or in a courtyard. Growing to 1 foot (30 cm) in height, it forms a clump of divided, deep green leaves and slender stems topped by nodding, cup-shaped flowers that are white with a pale pink tinge and prominent yellow stamens. ❀ **PLANTING** The Christmas rose should have quite rich, moist, and well-drained potting soil that has been enriched with additional organic matter, such as compost or manure, prior to planting. Mulch the soil surface to keep weed growth down. ❀ **FLOWERING** Flowers from late winter to early spring. The flowers remain attractive even after they have passed their peak. ❀ **CULTIVATION** Water routinely from spring onwards, but avoid allowing the pot to become saturated. Young foliage should be protected from snails and slugs, which can cause a lot of damage. Repot every four years or so, if necessary. ❀ **PROPAGATION** Either from seed sown in autumn, or by division of clumps in autumn or late winter.

Iberis sempervirens

Candytuft ○ ❖❖❖

✿ **OTHER NAME** Evergreen candytuft ✿ **DESCRIPTION** A delightful, low-growing evergreen perennial that is valued for its compact, trailing shape and wonderful display of white flowers in spring. A native of Europe and Asia, this plant will look particularly attractive in a container or hanging basket when positioned on a sunny, open balcony or verandah. Growing to 1 foot (30 cm) in height, it has a good covering of slender, oblong, dark green leaves and dense, rounded flower heads of tiny, pure-white flowers that look wonderful at dusk. ✿ **PLANTING** Choose a shallow pot or hanging basket filled with moderately rich, well-drained potting soil that has had all-purpose fertilizer added prior to planting. Water well, and keep in a shady place until established. ✿ **FLOWERING** Flowers from mid-spring to summer. ✿ **CULTIVATION** Water routinely during spring and summer, then reduce watering when the weather cools in autumn. Trim back after flowering to encourage a more dense growth, and feed with a liquid organic fertilizer in early spring to boost growth. ✿ **PROPAGATION** Either from seed in autumn, or from semi-ripe cuttings taken in summer.

Pelargonium species
Ivy leaf geranium ○ pH ❖

❀ **DESCRIPTION** There are many varieties of Pelargonium (geranium), but the ivy leaf geranium is probably the most suited to hanging baskets because of its delightful trailing habit. It is not to be confused with the true Geranium (Cranesbills). Ivy leaf geraniums are very useful, although tender, natives of South Africa which vary in size according to the variety. They have rounded, lobed leaves and bright semi-double or fully double flowers that bloom for long periods during the warmest time of the year. They can be grown in containers outdoors in temperate to warm climates, or brought indoors as house plants in cooler regions where the winters are too harsh. They dislike weather that is either too hot or too humid. ❀ **PLANTING** Use a light, friable, and well-drained potting mixture and make sure that the container has good drainage by lining the base with gravel or broken pieces of terracotta. Indeed, terracotta is an excellent style of pot for these plants, because it is porous and does not allow the potting soil to become waterlogged. ❀ **FLOWERING** In warm areas they will flower for eight months of the year or more, however, in cooler areas they flower from late spring until autumn. ❀ **CULTIVATION** Trim back growth in autumn to maintain a more compact shape. Water routinely in spring and summer, and dead-head frequently to encourage continuous flowering. Use a slow-release fertilizer to supply extra nutrients. ❀ **PROPAGATION** Easy to propagate from softwood cuttings taken from spring to autumn.

Penstemon davidsonii
Davidson penstemon ○ ❖❖❖

❀ **DESCRIPTION** A low-growing perennial with trailing stems that make a dense mat. It is usually grown as a ground cover, but is equally useful in a container or hanging basket positioned on a sunny balcony or verandah. Growing to 3 inches (7.5 cm) in height, it has small oval to rounded, dark green leathery leaves and a wonderful display of funnel-shaped flowers in the violet to red range. The variety 'Menziesii' is slightly taller in growth, with large, trumpet-shaped purple flowers. Grown in a container, it can be trained against a sunny wall. ❀ **PLANTING** The potting soil must be moderately rich and well drained, with some additional organic matter added. Choose a sunny, open position and water well until established.
❀ **FLOWERING** Flowers from late spring to midsummer.
❀ **CULTIVATION** Water routinely during spring and summer, and use an all-purpose, slow-release fertilizer in spring to boost growth.
❀ **PROPAGATION** From seed sown in spring or autumn, or by division of clumps in early spring. Semi-ripe cuttings can be taken in summer and early autumn.

Saponaria ocymoides

Soapwort ○ ❖❖❖

✿ **OTHER NAME:** Rock soapwort ✿ **DESCRIPTION** This plant is more often seen growing in a rockery garden or scree, however, it makes a very pretty pot plant if the correct growing conditions are provided. A common wild flower in Europe, it grows to 9 inches (22 cm) in height. It has a sprawling habit, with oval, hairy leaves and a profusion of small, flat flowers in the pale pink to crimson colour range. If well grown, the flowers should cover the entire plant and make a wonderful display. ✿ **PLANTING** The most suitable container would be a shallow terracotta bowl, providing the correct shape for the plant's sprawling habit as well as free drainage, because terracotta is porous. Line the base of the bowl with gravel or pieces of broken terracotta, and use a light, free-draining potting mixture. Position in a sunny, open situation. ✿ **FLOWERING** Flowers from late spring to early summer. ✿ **CULTIVATION** Water routinely, but take care not to overwater as soapwort can tolerate quite dry conditions and resents having wet feet. Trim back hard after flowering to prevent the plant from becoming leggy and shapeless. ✿ **PROPAGATION** Either from seed sown in autumn or spring, or from softwood cuttings taken in summer.

Saxifraga oppositifolia
Purple mountain saxifrage ○ ◐ ❖❖❖

❀ **DESCRIPTION** There are many varieties of *Saxifraga* that are suitable for containers and, indeed, often this form of cultivation is more successful than growing them directly in the ground. This species is a handsome, prostrate perennial with tiny leaves and masses of cup-shaped, dark purple, purple-pink and, occasionally, white flowers that cover the entire plant in early spring. It grows to only 2 inches (5 cm) in height, but can spread to more than 1 foot (30 cm), which makes it ideal for a shallow container. Grouped together with other alpine species, it can create a wonderful miniature garden.

❀ **PLANTING** This species should be positioned where it can receive sun, but not direct sunlight in the middle of the day. Use a moderately rich and moist potting soil, with some extra peat added, and ensure that the container provides good drainage, because although it likes moist soil conditions, it will resent being waterlogged. ❀ **FLOWERING** Flowers from early spring onwards. ❀ **CULTIVATION** Water routinely in spring and summer and reduce watering when the weather cools in winter.

❀ **PROPAGATION** Either from seed sown in autumn, or from rooted offsets in winter.

Silene vulgaris subsp. *maritima*

Sea campion   ○ ◐ ❖❖❖

✿ **DESCRIPTION** A low-growing, trailing plant that makes a pretty display in a shallow pot or hanging basket. Growing to only 1 inch (2.5 cm) in height, it has deep, spreading roots that assist it to cover the soil surface. The foliage is lance-shaped and grey-green, and the white flowers are soft with notched petals, making a pretty display. The variety 'Plena' has more bluish foliage, and double white, pompom-like flowers that are most attractive.
✿ **PLANTING** To produce good results, the Silene should have quite rich, fertile potting soil with extra well-rotted compost added. Make sure that the container has good drainage, and position it in either full sun or semi-shade. Water well until established, and mulch around the plant to prevent weed growth. ✿ **FLOWERING** Flowers from late spring to early summer. ✿ **CULTIVATION** Quite an easy plant to care for when established, it will require routine watering in spring and summer and all-purpose, slow-release fertilizer added in early spring to encourage good flower production. ✿ **PROPAGATION** Either from seed sown in autumn or spring, or from softwood cuttings taken in spring.

Viola odorata

English violet ◑ ● ❖❖❖

✿ **OTHER NAMES** Violet, Sweet violet ✿ **DESCRIPTION** One of the most popular and easy-to-grow perennials, the sweet violet is a charming addition to any old-fashioned garden. Valued for both its attractive foliage and flowers, the plant lends itself well to cultivation in a container. Growing to 8 inches (20 cm) in height, its rhizomatous roots spread quickly, filling the container and cascading over the sides. The dark green, glossy leaves are heart-shaped, while the dainty flowers are borne on slender stems, and can be violet or white in colour. There are many forms and cultivars, including 'Double Russian', which has double, deep purple blooms, and 'Royal Robe', which has purple flowers that are particularly fragrant. ✿ **PLANTING** The potting soil should be quite rich in humus and well-drained, capable of not drying out completely during hot, dry weather. Plant in autumn, and water well until seeds germinate or divisions take root. ✿ **FLOWERING** Flowers from late winter until mid-spring. ✿ **CULTIVATION** Water well if conditions are hot and dry, and protect foliage from snails and slugs which can be a problem. ✿ **PROPAGATION** Easy to propagate from seed in autumn or spring, or by division of clumps in autumn.

Allium cepa
Green bunching onions ○ ❖❖❖

✿ **OTHER NAMES** Shallots, Salad onions, Wild onions
✿ **DESCRIPTION** These members of the onion family are ideal for
growing in a container on a warm sunny balcony or verandah. They produce
tall, slender stems of green foliage, with white bulbs just beneath the soil
surface. ✿ **PLANTING** In spring sow the seed finely across the surface of
the potting soil, covering them lightly with some fine seed-raising mixture.
When they are 2 inches (5 cm) tall, thin out any that are too close together.
They will need quite rich potting mix, with some additional well-rotted manure
incorporated. ✿ **CULTIVATION** Water the potting mix daily in hot weather
to ensure steady growth. A sprinkling of all-purpose organic fertilizer after
four weeks will also boost growth. Remove any weeds that may appear, taking
care not to dislodge the onions. ✿ **HARVESTING** They are simply
harvested as you require them, by pulling them from the pot, roots and all.
It is better to pick them while they are still young and tender, as they will
become tough if left too long in the ground. Successive sowings will ensure
a steady supply. ✿ **PROPAGATION** From seed sown from spring
onwards.

Allium scheonoprasum

Chives ○ ❖❖❖

❀ **DESCRIPTION** This useful herb grows in a clump and looks very
attractive when grown in a terracotta herb pot on a sunny verandah or
balcony. Growing to 1 foot (30 cm) in height, it emerges from the soil as a
mass of slender, aromatic, grass-like green leaves that are topped by circular,
mauve flower heads. Chives are commonly used in salads and as a garnish to
many recipes. ❀ **PLANTING** To produce good results, sow the seed in
moderately rich, moist, and well-drained potting mixture that has been
enriched with additional compost or manure. Keep lightly moist until
germination. ❀ **CULTIVATION** Water every day if conditions are hot,
and sprinkle with an all-purpose fertilizer to encourage more lush growth.
❀ **HARVESTING** Simply clip the chives at ground level as required,
using clean, sharp scissors. Allow some stems to flower to provide seed for
the following season ❀ **PROPAGATION** From seed sown in spring, or
by division of clumps in early spring.

Anthriscus cerefolium

Chervil

✿ **OTHER NAME** French parsley ✿ **DESCRIPTION** This delightful herb has a distinctive, anise taste and can be used in a wide range of hot and cold recipes. It is a native of south-eastern Europe, growing to 18 inches (45 cm) in height, with slender stems covered with light-green, aromatic foliage that has a fine, feathery appearance. This foliage makes it an excellent potted herb for a sunny position anywhere in the garden. The small white flowers appear in midsummer, when the plant goes to seed.
✿ **PLANTING** Use a medium-size pot filled with moderately rich and well-drained potting mix, and sow the seeds finely on the surface, covering them with a fine layer of seed-raising mixture. Keep lightly watered until plants have germinated. ✿ **CULTIVATION** Water routinely in spring and summer, and pinch back the tops to prevent the plant from going to seed too rapidly. This will help keep it producing foliage for a little longer.
✿ **HARVESTING** Pick stems and leaves as required. Some stems can be allowed to flower and then go to seed to be gathered for sowing the following spring. ✿ **PROPAGATION** From seed sown in spring.

Capsicum annum

Peppers ○ ❖

✿ **OTHER NAMES** Bush peppers, Capsicum

✿ **DESCRIPTION** This tender plant is treated as an annual or glasshouse plant in most places but can be grown as a shrub in tropical areas. To produce ripe fruits it needs a long growing season, and will probably need to be started indoors in late winter. Growing to a height of 3 feet (1 m) when cultivated in a container, it has a good covering of mid-green leaves and will bear large, fleshy edible fruits varying in appearance, including yellow, purple, and red. ✿ **PLANTING** Sow seeds in some well-prepared seed-raising mixture on a sunny window ledge or in a glasshouse at the end of winter. Transplant into pots when the seedlings reach 6 inches (15 cm) in height, then take into the sun when all danger of frost has passed. A stake will be needed for support. Peppers are quite heavy feeders, so the potting mix should have some extra, rotted manure added prior to planting.

✿ **CULTIVATION** Water well, especially during summer, and feed with an all-purpose fertilizer when the flowers form to encourage good fruiting.

✿ **HARVESTING** Peppers can be picked and eaten after 12 weeks of growth, if they appear mature. Best eaten fresh. ✿ **PROPAGATION** By seed sown in late winter to early spring.

Citrus x *limonia*

Lemon ○ ❖

❖ **DESCRIPTION** Although not a hardy tree, the lemon is traditionally grown in Europe in large terracotta pots which are taken under shelter in winter. They are very decorative as a balcony or patio plant, and have a wonderful fragrance when in flower. Growing to 5 feet (1.5 m) when cultivated in a pot, lemon trees have masses of glossy green foliage, creamy flowers and edible fruits. ❖ **PLANTING** Lemons are quite demanding, and must have a good-quality, rich and moist potting mixture to produce good fruit. Add some well-rotted organic matter and a handful of specially formulated citrus food at planting time. Water well after potting, and mulch the surface of the pot to prevent the soil from drying out in summer.

❖ **CULTIVATION** Keep well watered during spring and summer, and feed with citrus food as the flowers and forming. Take care that the potting mixture does not dry out. Remove suckers that emerge from the base of the trunk, then prune out any dead wood from the centre as required.

❖ **HARVESTING** The fruits should be ready for picking from late summer onwards, depending on the climate. ❖ **PROPAGATION** By budding onto rootstock in autumn or spring.

Coriandrum sativum

Coriander ○ ❖❖❖

❀ **DESCRIPTION** A popular annual herb used in Asian and Indian recipes, coriander makes a pretty pot plant because of its delicate, feathery foliage. A native of southern Europe, coriander can grow to 3 feet (1 m) in height with tall stems of pale green foliage topped by delicate, white flower heads. The leaves, stems, and seeds are all edible, and have a very strong, distinctive aroma. ❀ **PLANTING** Use a medium-size container filled with quite rich, moist, and well-drained potting mixture. Sow the seeds lightly on the surface, then cover with a fine layer of seed-raising mixture. Water lightly until germination is successful. ❀ **CULTIVATION** Keep watering routinely, especially during hot, dry periods. A liquid organic fertilizer can be applied every three weeks or so to boost foliage growth. Keep weeds from around the plants as they will compete for moisture and nutrients. ❀ **HARVESTING** Cut stems or foliage and use fresh as required. Allow some stems of the plant to flower and go to seed, so that the seeds can be collected and then dried for a more concentrated taste. ❀ **PROPAGATION** From seed sown in spring.

Cucurbita pepo

Courgette ○ ❖❖❖

✿ **OTHER NAME** Zucchini ✿ **DESCRIPTION** There are many varieties that can be grown in a large tub or pot, making a pretty display on a sunny balcony or verandah or in a conservatory. It is a smooth-skinned squash that should only be eaten when young and tender, and can be used in a wide variety of recipes. It can grow to 3 feet (1 m) in size, with slender, spiky stems topped by large leaves. Small stalks emerge from the base with brilliant, yellow flowers from which the fruits develop. The flowers are also edible. There are dark and light green, grey, and yellow varieties, all of which are very easy-to-grow. ✿ **PLANTING** Choose a medium to large container filled with rich, moist, and well-drained potting mixture. Add a handful of all-purpose fertilizer at the time of planting the seeds, in early spring. Only plant two seeds per pot, and when the seedlings emerge, remove the weakest one. ✿ **CULTIVATION** Plenty of water will be needed to keep the plant growing quickly. A liquid organic fertilizer every three weeks will also give a boost. Check plants daily for the fruits, which grow very rapidly in warm weather. ✿ **HARVESTING** Pick the fruits when they are no more than 10 in (25 cm) in length, or even smaller for more tender fruits. ✿ **PROPAGATION** From seed sown in spring.

Lactuca sativa

Lettuce ○ ❖❖❖

✿ **DESCRIPTION** Several of the smaller varieties of lettuce can be easily grown in a large container or trough, providing fresh salad vegetables from the garden. Look for seed or seedlings of mignonette, butter, or cos lettuce, which take up only a small amount of space for the yield supplied. Cos lettuce has rather an upright growth habit, which is very space-saving, while the other small lettuces can be grown very close together and will produce results in as little as six weeks during warm weather. ✿ **PLANTING** A trough or window box in a sunny position are ideal for growing lettuce. The potting mix must be rich, moist, and well drained with some added organic matter and all-purpose fertilizer incorporated prior to planting the seed or seedlings.

✿ **CULTIVATION** Water routinely, especially during hot weather, as the plants will slow down in their growth and become tough if the potting soil dries out. Use a liquid organic fertilizer every three weeks to keep growth rapid. Watch out for snails and slugs which can damage young plants quite severely. ✿ **HARVESTING** Pick and eat when young and tender, or harvest leaves one at a time for a few weeks before picking the heart. Harvest before the plants bolt to seed in midsummer. Successive plantings will ensure a steady supply. ✿ **PROPAGATION** From seed sown from spring onwards.

Lycopersicon esculentum
Tomatoes ○ ❖❖❖

✿ **DESCRIPTION** One of the most successful crops for a large tub or container, many of the smaller varieties of tomato are the most adaptable for this purpose. Tomatoes need a long, hot summer for their fruits to ripen, which is why the smaller salad tomatoes or egg tomatoes are better in cooler areas, because they take far less time to mature. Pots of tomatoes can be positioned in any sunny part of the garden, or on a balcony or verandah that gets sun for most of the day. ✿ **PLANTING** Raise seed to seedling stage under glass or on a sunny window ledge in late winter, transplanting them into good size pots when they reach 6 inches (15 cm) in height. Take outside into a sunny position when all chance of frost has passed. Insert a small stake at the time of transplanting, to provide support as the plants grow. A rich, well-drained potting mix is essential, with plenty of organic matter added. ✿ **CULTIVATION** Water routinely as the plants grow, and use a specially formulated tomato fertilizer as a side-dressing every three or four weeks. Tie up the plants to the stake as they grow, and pinch out lateral growths to prevent a leggy shape and to encourage more flowers and fruit. ✿ **HARVESTING** Allow the fruit to ripen on the plant, or if very late in the season, pick and ripen in a warm place. ✿ **PROPAGATION** From seed sown in early spring.

Ocimum basilicum

Basil ○ ❖❖❖

❀ **DESCRIPTION** A charming herb for a warm, sunny position, that will look best when planted in a traditional terracotta pot. Basil must have plenty of warmth to grow well, and can only be grown in summer in many regions. Native to the hotter parts of the Mediterranean, basil is a leafy plant, growing to 2 feet (60 cm). It forms a pleasant shape with mid-green, oval leaves that have a strong, distinctive aroma when crushed. Basil is used in a wide range of hot and cold recipes, and it can also be dried and stored for later use. ❀ **PLANTING** Choose a sunny, open position and scatter seeds on the surface of a good-quality, well-drained potting mixture. Cover with a fine layer of seed-raising mixture, and water well until germination.

❀ **CULTIVATION** Keep the plant well watered, especially if conditions are hot and dry. Pinch out the centre bud as the plants grow to encourage a more leafy, compact shape. Doing this, the plant should last for most of the summer. ❀ **HARVESTING** Simply pick off foliage as required. When drying, hang bunches in a dry, dark place for several weeks before crushing and storing in an airtight jar. ❀ **PROPAGATION** From seed sown in spring.

Raphanus sativus

Radish ○ ❖❖❖

❀ **DESCRIPTION** The fastest growing of all vegetables, the radish will not make a pretty display; however, it is handy to grow them in a pot or trough near the kitchen where they can be plucked at will. There are several varieties of radish, including the round cherry radishes, and Asian varieties with long, slender white roots. All are suited to container cultivation.

❀ **PLANTING** The seed of the radish is very small, and it will need to be scattered on the surface of moderately rich, well-drained potting mixture, then covered with a fine layer of seed-raising mixture. Water daily until the seeds germinate, then thin out to a distance of 2 inches (5 cm) apart when the seedlings are large enough to handle. The potting soil does not need to be rich with manure, and should ideally have some lime incorporated prior to planting. ❀ **CULTIVATION** Keep watering routinely, as radishes must be grown rapidly or they become tough and woody. Remove weeds as they appear, because they will compete for moisture and nutrients.

❀ **HARVESTING** Depending on the variety, the first radishes should be ready after four of five weeks from the sowing of the seed. Pick them alternately, and make sure they do not remain in the ground too long. Successive sowing will ensure a steady supply. ❀ **PROPAGATION** From seed sown from spring onwards.

Rosmarinus officinalis

Rosemary ○ ❖❖❖

❀ **DESCRIPTION** This evergreen shrub that grows to about 3 feet (1 m) high. The flowers are mauve, or blue, and scented, but the small, linear leaves give the plant its wonderfully-pungent reputation. Rosemary is frequently used for cooking, and should be positioned near the kitchen for easy access. It is also attractive to bees. ❀ **PLANTING** A sunny position is preferred, although light shade can be tolerated. Some protection from wind is also desirable. Plant at any time of year into quite rich, moist and well-drained potting mix, to which extra humus has been added. ❀ **FLOWERING** The first flowers appear during spring, carrying through until summer. ❀ **CULTIVATION** Rosemary requires very little attention once established. The potting mix should be kept just moist, as too much water will shorten the length of its life. An application of compost and blood and bone during spring is beneficial. Slow-release fertilizer will also do the trick. Little pruning is required except to remove any straggly growth. Although this is best carried out during autumn, frost-damaged wood may be removed during early spring. ❀ **PROPAGATION** Take heeled cuttings during summer, autumn, or winter from strong side shoots. Bottom heat will speed up the striking process.

Solanum melongena esculentum
Aubergine ○ ❖❖❖

❀ **OTHER NAME** Eggplant ❀ **DESCRIPTION** This vegetable needs a long, hot summer for the fruits to mature; however, it makes a handsome container plant that is ideal for a warm, sunny balcony or verandah and they can be grown in a conservatory or greenhouse. There are some smaller-growing varieties that will be ready for harvesting in a much shorter space of time. Growing to 3 feet (1 m) in a pot, they have mid-green leaves and violet-purple flowers followed by purple, white, or yellow fruits, according to the variety. ❀ **PLANTING** To get the plants off to a good start, raise them to seedling stage under glass or on a sunny windowsill in late winter. Transplant into quite large containers when the seedlings are 6 inches (15 cm) in height, but do not put them outside until all danger of frost has passed. The potting soil will need to be quite rich, moist, and well drained, and a stake should be provided to support the plants as they grow. ❀ **CULTIVATION** Water routinely, and keep weeds from growing around the base of the plant. After four weeks growth apply some specially formulated tomato fertilizer, which will provide the correct nutrient balance for healthy growth. ❀ **HARVESTING** You may have to wait up to five or six months for harvesting, depending on the warmth of the summer. ❀ **PROPAGATION** From seed sown under glass in late winter or early spring.

Thymus vulgaris

Garden thyme ○ ❖❖❖

✿ **DESCRIPTION** One of the most popular and easy-to-grow aromatic perennial herbs, which can be cultivated in many ways. Thyme is an excellent potted plant, cascading over the edge of the container. Locate it near an outdoor entertaining area where its fragrance can be easily enjoyed. It is also an important inclusion in the potted herb garden. Thyme is a low-growing, ground-covering herb with slender stems and masses of tiny, evergreen greyish leaves that are highly aromatic. For many weeks in summer it is covered with small, lilac-purple flowers that are borne on small, upright spikes.

✿ **PLANTING** The best position is in full sun, and the potting soil needs to be reasonably fertile, with good drainage. Plenty of well-rotted compost and manure should be added to the potting mix to lift and aerate it, to provide extra nutrients, and to help retain moisture. ✿ **FLOWERING** Flowers bloom over many months from early summer. ✿ **CULTIVATION** Mulch around plants to keep the soil surface free from weeds, and to help prevent the ground from drying out in summer. Water during dry weather, and prune lightly in spring if stems become lax or straggly.

✿ **PROPAGATION** From semi-ripe or softwood cuttings taken in summer.

Anemone blanda
Greek anemone ○ ◑ ❖❖❖

✿ **DESCRIPTION** A charming, tuberous-rooted perennial plant that is valued because its flowers appear in winter, when little else is happening in the garden. Ideal for a shallow pot or window box, it grows to 8 inches (20 cm) in height, and has attractive oval, mid-green leaves that are deeply toothed. The leaves are held semi-erect, and there are upright stems that hold flattish, deep blue, pink, or white flowers that make a pretty display. Useful varieties include 'White Splendour', which has open flowers with white petals and yellow stamens; 'Atrocaerulea', which has wonderful deep blue flowers; and 'Radar', with carmine-red flowers with a pale eye.

✿ **PLANTING** To grow successfully the potting soil must be rich in humus, so add some well-rotted compost or manure prior to planting. Water well, and maintain this regime as anemones like quite moist soil conditions. ✿ **FLOWERING** Flowers appear from midwinter onwards.

✿ **CULTIVATION** Apart from routine watering, very little attention is required. Repot every four years if necessary. ✿ **PROPAGATION** From division of clumps in spring, or by seed sown in late summer. Root cuttings can also be taken in winter.

Crinum asiaticum
Grand crinum ○ ❖❖

✿ **DESCRIPTION** A member of the Amaryllis family and native to
tropical regions of the world, crinum is a tender, herbaceous plant. It will
make a pretty potted plant that must be taken under cover during winter in
cool to cold climates. Growing to 18 inches (45 cm) in height, it forms a
handsome clump of dark green, glossy, strap-like leaves. From the centre of
the clump emerges slender stems topped by unusual white flowers with
long, fine petals. ✿ **PLANTING** Provide quite a rich, moist potting soil
by adding extra compost or well-rotted manure prior to planting. Use a
medium-size container, and make sure the drainage is adequate by placing
gravel or pieces of broken terracotta in the base. Position in a sunny but
sheltered place, and water well until established. ✿ **FLOWERING** Flowers
either in spring or summer. ✿ **CULTIVATION** Water routinely, but
ensure that the potting soil is never waterlogged. After the flowers die
back, feed with an all-purpose, slow-release fertilizer to encourage
flowering the following season. Reduce watering in autumn and winter.
✿ **PROPAGATION** From offsets or seed in spring.

Crocus species

Crocus ○ ◑ ❖❖❖

✿ **DESCRIPTION** These are among the most enchanting of all the flowering bulbs, making delightful potted plants positioned in a warm, sheltered area of the garden or balcony. There are many varieties from which to choose, all quite small-growing at about 3 to 6 inches (7 to 15 cm) in height. Most emerge from the ground by producing their tubular flowers prior to the appearance of the slender, mid-green, strap-like foliage. Flower colours vary from white and palest lilac to brilliant yellow, orange-yellow, pink, and purple. Crocuses make the best display when planted in a broad, shallow container or window box. ✿ **PLANTING** Use a rich, moist potting soil that is well drained, or a potting mixture that has been specially formulated for bulbs. Position in semi-shade in warmer areas, and full sun if the climate is cool. ✿ **FLOWERING** Most varieties flower from late winter to early autumn. ✿ **CULTIVATION** Water routinely, taking care not to overwater in autumn and winter. Sprinkle with an all-purpose, slow-release fertilizer after the flowers have finished, to encourage good flowering the following season. ✿ **PROPAGATION** Easily propagated by division of clumps in early autumn.

Cyclamen hederifolium
Neapolitan cyclamen ○ ◑ ❖❖❖

✿ **OTHER NAME** Cyclamen ✿ **DESCRIPTION** Cyclamens are charming plants that may be difficult to establish; however, once they have nestled into a comfortable position they will require very little care and attention. Growing to 4 inches (10 cm) in height, the Neapolitan cyclamen forms an attractive clump of ivy-shaped, bright green foliage, often with silver-green markings. The flowers are absolutely delightful, held above the foliage on slender stems, and are pale to deep pink. Cyclamens can be planted in a shallow terracotta pot that will display their beauty, while also providing the correct growing conditions. The flowers and foliage die back in winter.
✿ **PLANTING** Cyclamens require moderately rich, light, and well-drained potting mix. The trick with cyclamens is to only water them during the active growing period, from autumn into winter. Otherwise, the potting mixture should be allowed to remain quite dry. ✿ **FLOWERING** Flowers appear in late autumn. ✿ **CULTIVATION** It is essential that cyclamens are allowed to dry out in summer. In autumn they can be restarted by transplanting into a new container with fresh potting soil, followed by routine watering to activate growth. ✿ **PROPAGATION** From seed in late summer or autumn.

Hyacinthus orientalis
Hyacinth ○ ◑ ❖❖❖

❀ **DESCRIPTION** This beautiful, fragrant plant is one of the best bulbs for container cultivation. Pots can be moved around in outdoor living areas, where the strong fragrance can be easily enjoyed. Growing to a height of 15 inches (38 cm), hyacinths have tall spikes of waxy, bell-shaped flowers that emerge from the ground before the basal leaves. There are many varieties and hybrids to choose from, including 'Delft Blue', which has soft blue flowers flushed with violet; 'Ostara', which has blue flowers with a deep purple stripe along each petal; and 'Pink Pearl', which has dense spikes of carmine-pink flowers. There are also some excellent white forms available.
❀ **PLANTING** Use a moderately rich, well-drained potting mixture with some extra well-rotted organic matter added. Position in a sunny or semi-shaded situation, with shelter from strong winds. ❀ **FLOWERING** Flowers from late winter to early spring. ❀ **CULTIVATION** Take care not to overwater, but do not allow the potting mixture to dry out completely. After the flowers die back, apply an all-purpose fertilizer to encourage good blooms the following season. ❀ **PROPAGATION** From offsets in late summer or early autumn.

Ipheion uniflorum

Spring starflower ○ ◑ ❖❖❖

❀ **DESCRIPTION** Starflowers are a charming group of small bulbs that can be grown in containers with great success, creating a pretty display of starry flowers in early spring. Growing to 10 inches (25 cm) in height, the plant forms a clump of slender, pale green leaves that have a strange onion aroma if crushed. From the foliage emerge slender stems topped by delicate, starry flowers in the pale to dark blue colour range. The variety 'Wisley Blue' has particularly attractive deep blue blooms. ❀ **PLANTING** Use a shallow, broad container and sow the bulbs in autumn to create a dense clump. The potting mix should be light and well drained, yet still contain sufficient organic matter to retain moisture during summer. Add a handful of well-rotted compost prior to planting. Place in a semi-shaded position for the first few weeks, then bring into the sun during winter. ❀ **FLOWERING** Flowers appear in early spring. ❀ **CULTIVATION** Water routinely, taking care not to overwater as, like most bulbs, they resent very damp conditions. After flowering has died back, feed with an all-purpose fertilizer and allow the foliage to completely wither and die. Reduce watering over summer. ❀ **PROPAGATION** By offsets in early autumn.

Narcissus species
Daffodil ○ ◑ ❖❖❖

❀ **DESCRIPTION** Probably the most popular of all flowering bulbs, the
daffodil makes an excellent plant for a container to brighten up any balcony
or verandah during spring. The flowers vary considerably according to the
variety, from white to deepest yellow. The trumpets also vary in colour and
shape, some in beautiful shades of apricot-pink to orange. The stems are
erect and hollow, reaching 12 to 18 inches (30 to 45 cm) in height, while
the leaves are dark green and rush-like. There are hundreds of different
varieties of daffodil, with flower forms including large cupped, double,
miniature, and those with reflexed petals. ❀ **PLANTING** Use a moderately
rich, well-drained potting mix and plant the bulbs in autumn for a spring
display. The trick with growing bulbs in a container is to keep them in the
dark for a few weeks after planting, bringing them out only when winter has
started. For a pretty display, plant the bulbs in a clump in a shallow, bowl-
shaped container. Afterwards, mulch with compost or leaf litter.
❀ **FLOWERING** Flowers appear from late winter through to early spring.
❀ **CULTIVATION** Begin feeding with a balanced fertilizer after the
blooms have faded. Allow the bulbs to remain undisturbed for several years
until they become congested. When necessary, lift and divide and repot during
autumn. Keep the soil moist throughout summer but take care not to
overwater. Daffodils may be attacked by eelworms, the narcissus fly, bulb rot,
or rust. ❀ **PROPAGATION** By dividing offsets in autumn.

Tulipa hybrids
Tulip ○ ❖

✿ **DESCRIPTION** In a shallow container positioned in a sunny courtyard or on a balcony, tulips always put on a spectacular display and are among the most highly prized spring-flowering bulbs. They come in a tremendous range of colours, sizes, and shapes. The stem-length too, varies in height from 10 to 32 inches (25 to 80 cm). They may be pink, apricot, red, yellow, black, or combinations thereof. Tulips will always have the classic cup shape, however, and characteristic, grey-green leaves.

✿ **PLANTING** Mid-autumn to early winter, plant the bulbs 5 to 6 inches (12 to 15 cm) deep in light, fertile, and well-drained potting mixture. It is best to keep the container in a dark place, or cover the top of the pot to preclude light for several weeks after planting. Bring out into the sun during winter. ✿ **FLOWERING** Flowers from early to mid-spring, depending on the variety. ✿ **CULTIVATION** Remove blooms as they fade and keep the potting soil well watered throughout the summer season. An application of complete fertilizer is also beneficial at this time. When the leaves have completely died down, lift the bulbs and store in dry peat moss until the following autumn. In warmer climates, it may be necessary to chill the bulbs in the refrigerator for six to eight weeks. When in flower, keep your eye out for aphids. ✿ **PROPAGATION** From seed or bulblets divided in autumn.

Ageratum houstonianum
Floss flower ○

✿ **DESCRIPTION** A fast-growing annual with wonderful, fluffy flower heads that make a great display in a window box or pot in a sunny position on a balcony or in a courtyard garden. Growing to 1 foot (30 cm) in height, there are also much smaller cultivars that are more compact in their growth habit. The foliage is mid-green and oval-shaped, and the blooms emerge as feathery flower heads in various shades of blue, pink, and white. Useful varieties include 'Blue Danube', which is small-growing and has clear blue flowers; 'Pinkie', which is a taller variety with soft pink flowers; and 'White Cushion', which has attractive white blooms. ✿ **PLANTING** This plant likes quite a rich, moist potting mix that has had some extra organic matter added prior to planting. It can be grown from seeds or seedlings, planted in spring in cooler areas and in autumn in warm to tropical regions. Water well until established. ✿ **FLOWERING** Flowers from midsummer to autumn, depending on when the seeds were sown. ✿ **CULTIVATION** Water routinely as the plants grow, and keep weeds from competing around the base of the plants. Dead-head regularly to encourage continuous flowering. ✿ **PROPAGATION** From seed sown in autumn or spring.

Calendula officinalis

Pot marigold ○

✿ **OTHER NAME** Calendula ✿ **DESCRIPTION** This is one of the
easiest and most successful annuals to grow in a container positioned on a
sunny balcony or verandah. The original species has bright orange, daisy or
chrysanthemum-like blooms. New strains are available, however, in yellow,
gold, cream, and white. The pot marigold can reach 1½ to 2 feet (45 to 60
cm) in height and width, but dwarf forms are also available. The pale green
leaves produce a rather pungent odour that is not always appreciated, while
the blooms are sweetly scented. Containers of pot marigolds can be grouped
together with other flowering annuals to create a stunning display.

✿ **PLANTING** Pot marigolds thrive in moist, fertile, and well-drained
potting mix that has been enriched with added organic matter. They require
full sun and the seedlings need to be spaced 12 to 15 inches (30 to 38 cm)
apart at planting time. ✿ **FLOWERING** Flowers from spring through to
autumn. ✿ **CULTIVATION** Ensure that the plants are kept moist and
well fed with a liquid organic fertilizer throughout the growing season. After
the first blooms have faded, clip them back to encourage a second flush. These
flowers should be allowed to self-seed during autumn if you wish to see them
again the following year. Remove any plants that become infected with powdery
mildew or the cucumber mosaic virus. ✿ **PROPAGATION** By seed sown
in early spring through to early summer.

Cheiranthus cheirii

Wallflower ○ p̂H

✿ **OTHER NAME** English wallflower ✿ **DESCRIPTION** A delightful, fragrant plant that is ideal for growing in a container or tub in an open, sunny situation. During spring, numerous single blooms appear on tall spikes in shades of red, orange, yellow, brown, and white. The leaves are lance-shaped and dull green in appearance. There are tall, intermediate, and dwarf varieties that range from 8 inches to 2 feet (20 to 60 cm) in height. Dwarf varieties are well-suited to small containers, while the taller types look best when used as a background plant in a mixed grouping.
✿ **PLANTING** Choose an open, sunny position and use a well-drained, moderately rich potting mix. Neutral to alkaline potting soil is essential, so add a sprinkling of dolomite lime prior to planting. Plant seedlings during late autumn or early winter. ✿ **FLOWERING** Flowers from spring through to summer, depending on the time of planting.
✿ **CULTIVATION** Keep moist throughout spring and summer, but not wet. Liquid fertilizer can be applied every two weeks to produce larger blooms. Remove flower spikes as they fade to encourage further flowering, or allow them to go to seed to be gathered for the following spring. ✿ **PROPAGATION** By seed sown during late spring or early summer.

Coleus blumei
Coleus ◑

✿ **DESCRIPTION** A charming, old-fashioned foliage plant that will look very pretty in a container positioned in dappled light outdoors or indoors in bright light as a houseplant. Coleus is valued for its dramatic leaves, which may be purple, red, pink, green, and yellow and very showy. The leaves vary considerably in size and shape and have a rather velvety texture. The flowers appear in spikes during summer, and should be pinched out immediately to encourage further foliage growth. ✿ **PLANTING** One of the joys of this plant is its ease of cultivation. It can be grown simply from stem cuttings placed into any average potting soil, with its main requirement being plenty of moisture if conditions are hot and dry. ✿ **FLOWERING** Insignificant flowers appear in summer. ✿ **CULTIVATION** Water routinely, and position the plants so they do not get direct sunlight on their leaves, especially during midsummer. Keep pinching back flowers to encourage a more bushy shape. When grown as houseplants they need quite severe pruning to prevent leggy growth. ✿ **PROPAGATION** A very easy plant to propagate from softwood cuttings taken in spring or summer, or from seed sown in late winter under glass.

Cosmos bipinnatus

Cosmos ○

✿ **DESCRIPTION** An easy-to-grow annual that has outstanding showy flowers that will look marvellous in a container positioned on a sunny verandah or balcony. Cosmos is a quite tall-growing plant, up to 2 feet (60 cm) in height, and should therefore be placed in a pot at the back of a mixed grouping for a lovely summer display. This plant is admired for its feathery, mid-green leaves, which look quite pretty even before the flowers emerge. The blooms are large and pink, although there are also varieties in white and deep crimson. Useful forms include 'Purity', which has pure-white flowers; and 'Sensation', which has red, pink, and white flowers. ✿ **PLANTING** Cosmos will thrive in any moderately rich, moist, and well-drained potting soil. Sow the seed or seedlings in spring or autumn, depending on the climate. Water well until established.
✿ **FLOWERING** Flowers from summer through to autumn, depending on when the seeds were sown. ✿ **CULTIVATION** Water regularly in spring and summer, and watch for snails and slugs which can damage the young foliage. ✿ **PROPAGATION** From seed, which should be sown in autumn in temperate to tropical regions, and in spring in cool to cold climates.

Eschscholzia californica

Californian poppy ○

✿ **DESCRIPTION** Given a little attention, these fast-growing annuals put on a stunning display with their delicate foliage and colourful flowers, and make attractive container plants. The first thing you notice about them are the curious little hats that protect the developing blooms. Traditionally, the flowers are orange and have a satiny appearance, but nowadays, Californian poppies come in a variety of shades, including pink, yellow, cream, and red. There are also dwarf forms with small, bright yellow blooms. The grey-green, fern-like leaves are also attractive, and develop on 1 foot (30 cm) stems.

✿ **PLANTING** Californian poppies do not like being transplanted, so it is best to sow the seed direct during autumn or early spring. A light, well-drained potting mixture is preferable, in an open, sunny position. Once the seedlings have emerged, thin out the surplus ones, leaving 6 inch (15 cm) spacings, and keep them moist and protect emerging seedlings from snails.

✿ **FLOWERING** From summer through to the end of autumn, depending on when the seed is sown. ✿ **CULTIVATION** The potting mix should be kept just moist throughout summer, and the spent flowers should be removed for a longer display. Left alone, the Californian poppy will self-seed freely and will re-emerge the following season.

✿ **PROPAGATION** By seed from early spring onwards.

Impatiens hybrids

Balsam ○ ◑

✿ **OTHER NAME** Busy lizzie ✿ **DESCRIPTION** These attractive
perennials are generally grown as annuals, because they will not survive
through the winter in most climates. They are succulent plants, growing to
2 feet (60 cm) in height, with attractive, pointed, green or bronze-green
foliage. Sometimes the foliage is also variegated with yellow or white markings.
The flowers are particularly bright and vibrant. They are flat, open blooms
in various shades of red, cerise, orange, and pink. The New Guinea hybrids
are particularly striking, many with marbled foliage and flowers. All varieties
make excellent plants for containers, positioned in a warm, sheltered
courtyard or balcony garden. ✿ **PLANTING** To grow successfully, either
in full sun or partial shade, balsam must have moderately rich, moist, and
well-drained potting soil. Plant the seed or seedlings in spring, and keep
damp until they are well established. ✿ **FLOWERING** Flowers from late
spring through summer. ✿ **CULTIVATION** Water well, especially if
conditions are hot and dry. Mulch to keep weeds from competing and to
help prevent the soil from drying out. Red spider mites and aphids can be a
problem. ✿ **PROPAGATION** Either from seed sown in spring, or from
stem cuttings taken in summer.

Lathyrus odoratus

Sweet pea ○ pH

✿ **DESCRIPTION** Sweet peas make a charming display, and are commonly grown for their delightfully fragrant blooms. They are tendril-climbing annuals with mid-green foliage, which can reach a height of 5 to 10 feet (1.5 to 3 m) in the right conditions. The blooms are profuse and come in blue, mauve, red, pink, and white shades. The attractive petals are normally ruffled and may be two-toned or mottled in appearance. They can be grown in a trough or tub against a trellis to create a pretty summer display.

✿ **PLANTING** In mild areas, sow the seed direct from late summer to autumn. Choose a position that receives full sun. For faster germination, soak the seeds in water for a couple of hours prior to planting. Prepare the potting mixture by incorporating generous amounts of compost and complete fertilizer. Acid soils will also require a dressing of lime. Before sowing, erect a mesh or wire support against the chosen wall or fence to provide the necessary support. In cooler climates, sow in spring for a summer display.

✿ **FLOWERING** Flowers appear from spring through to late summer.

✿ **CULTIVATION** Keep plants well watered during summer, and feed regularly with liquid fertilizer. Mulching is also beneficial. To develop strong side branches, pinch the seedlings back when they reach 4 inches. (10 cm) high. The blooms are ideal for vase arrangements and should be picked regularly to encourage further blooms. ✿ **PROPAGATION** From seed sown in late summer to autumn.

Lobelia erinus
Edging lobelia ○ ◑

✿ **DESCRIPTION** Edging lobelia is a popular and easy-to-grow annual
with intense blue flowers that is ideal for use in containers, window boxes,
and hanging baskets. It grows to a height of 4 to 8 inches (10 to 20 cm) with
a spread of 4 to 6 inches (10 to 15 cm) and flowers over a long period. Trailing
and more compact types are available, and there are new varieties, including
white, wine-red, pink, and mauve. The pale green leaves may be oval or lance-
shaped, and some have a bronze tinge. ✿ **PLANTING** Seedlings are best
planted out during early spring into rich, moist, and well-drained potting
soil. The addition of compost and manure prior to planting will produce
better blooms. A sunny position is preferred, however, edging lobelia can
also tolerate part shade, particularly in warmer regions. The seedlings should
be spaced 4 to 6 inches (10 to 15 cm) apart. ✿ **FLOWERING** Flowers
from late spring through to autumn. ✿ **CULTIVATION** Water regularly
throughout the growing season, and once flowering has commenced apply
liquid fertilizer every two weeks. When the blooms have faded, they disperse
their seed and the plant slowly withers. The plants should be pulled out at
this stage. ✿ **PROPAGATION** By seed sown in spring and summer.

Nemesia strumosa

Nemesia ○

✿ **DESCRIPTION** A delightful, fast-growing, bushy annual that makes a pretty pot plant on a sunny balcony or patio. Growing to 18 inches (45 cm) in height, it will maintain a more pleasant, bushy shape if pinched back regularly when young. This species has pale green, lance-shaped leaves with serrated edges, and showy trumpet-shaped flowers that are yellow, white, blue, or purple. They make excellent cut flowers for indoor arrangements. Useful varieties include 'Blue Gem', which has porcelain-blue flowers, and the Carnival Series, which has yellow, purple, orange, red, and white flowers.

✿ **PLANTING** Plant seeds or seedlings into moderately rich, moist, and well-drained potting soil. If growing from seed, cover with a fine layer of seed-raising mixture and keep lightly damp until germination. Position in a sunny, open situation. ✿ **FLOWERING** Flowers from mid-spring onwards, depending on when the seeds were sown. ✿ **CULTIVATION** Water routinely, especially when conditions are hot and dry, and pinch back tips to keep the shape of the plants bushy. Cut back stems after flowering.

✿ **PROPAGATION** From seed sown in spring in cool climates, or in early autumn in temperate regions.

Nicotiana alata (syn. *Nicotiana affinis*)
Flowering tobacco ○ ◑

✿ **DESCRIPTION** This attractive, rosette-forming perennial is generally grown as an annual, making a pleasant display at the back of a mixed grouping of pots. Growing to 3 feet (1 m) or more in height, it has oval, mid-green leaves and clusters of tubular, cream-white flowers that exude a pleasant fragrance in the evening. There is also a green form, 'Lime Green', which has a similar although slightly more compact growth habit, and the Sensation Series, which has pointed leaves and rose or crimson flowers. ✿ **PLANTING** Position pots in either full sun or dappled shade, and use a moderately rich, moist, and well-drained potting mix. If growing from seed, plants can be raised to seedling stage in punnets, then transplanted into larger pots when 6 inches (15 cm) in height. ✿ **FLOWERING** Flowers from summer to early autumn, depending on when the seeds were sown.

✿ **CULTIVATION** Keep these plants well watered, especially during spring and summer if conditions are hot and dry. An application of liquid organic fertilizer after six weeks growth will help to boost flower production. ✿ **PROPAGATION** From seed sown in autumn in temperate regions, or in spring in cool climates.

Nigella damascena

Love-in-the-mist ○

✿ **OTHER NAME** Love-in-a-mist ✿ **DESCRIPTION** An easy-to-grow
and pretty annual that is a member of the buttercup family, and native to
southern Europe. It has most attractive foliage and flowers, and makes a very
decorative pot plant positioned in full sun. It is a fast-growing species,
reaching 18 inches (45 cm) in height, with slender, upright stems clothed in
fine, feathery, bright green foliage. The spurred flowers are small but showy
semi-doubles in shades of blue, pink, and white. Worthwhile varieties include
'Miss Jekyll', which has semi-double blue flowers, and 'Persian Jewels', which
has white, pink, or purple-blue flowers. The flowers are followed by decorative
seed pods, which can be dried to provide seed for the following season.
✿ **PLANTING** This annual grows well in average potting soil providing
drainage is adequate. Add some organic matter to the mix prior to sowing the
seeds, and keep the potting soil lightly moist until germination.
✿ **FLOWERING** Flowers during late spring and early summer.
✿ **CULTIVATION** Water routinely during spring and early summer, and
weed around the young seedlings as they grow. A mulch layer will help to
keep the soil moist, and dead-heading will encourage more flowers to be
produced. ✿ **PROPAGATION** In cool climates, sow the seed in spring
when the danger of frost has passed; in other regions, sow the seed in autumn.

Petunia hybrids

Petunia ph ○

✿ **OTHER NAME** Common garden petunia ✿ **DESCRIPTION**
Petunias are one of the most easily cultivated of annuals, with fast foliage
growth and masses of blooms in an amazing variety, including pink, white,
red, purple, yellow, blue, and salmon shades. Two-tone combinations are also
very popular. Dwarf types reach from 6 to 8 inches (15 to 20 cm), while
taller varieties may grow as high as 1 foot (30 cm). Many are scented,
although some of the new varieties have lost this attribute. They look most
effective growing in a container or hanging basket, with their foliage
cascading over the sides. ✿ **PLANTING** Plant seedlings during early spring
into a sunny position with moist, well-drained potting mix. A little lime
should be added if the soil is on the acid side. ✿ **FLOWERING** Flowers
from summer through to autumn. ✿ **CULTIVATION** Petunias need to
be watered regularly throughout the growing season, but go easy on the
nitrogenous fertilizer to prevent excessive foliage growth at the expense of
the flowers. Phosphorous-based fertilizers will often give better results.
Faded blooms should be pinched off regularly with your fingertips to extend
the flowering period. Lightly trim the plants during late summer to induce
an autumn flush. Virus-infected petunias should be removed immediately.
✿ **PROPAGATION** By seed sown under glass during early spring.

Tagetes erecta
African marigold ○

✿ **OTHER NAME** Aztec marigold ✿ **DESCRIPTION** A fast-growing, upright and bushy annual that grows well in pots if positioned in full sun. Reaching 2 feet (60 cm) in height, there are also medium and dwarf varieties, which are even more suited to container cultivation. African marigolds have deeply divided, glossy, deep green leaves with an aroma that some people do not find particularly pleasing. The flowers are large and showy, forming semi-circular, double heads of petals in the yellow, orange, and bronze-red range. Worthwhile varieties include the Inca Series, which is a group of dwarf plants mixed in gold, orange, and yellow; and 'Crackerjack', which is a tall variety with large, double yellow or orange blooms. ✿ **PLANTING** Easy-to-grow in any moderately rich, well-drained potting soil, African marigolds can either be raised from seed or planted out as seedlings. Water well until established. ✿ **FLOWERING** Flowers from summer to autumn, depending on when the seed was sown. ✿ **CULTIVATION** Water routinely during the main growing periods of spring and summer. Dead-head spent flowers to encourage the production of more blooms, and protect plants from snails and slugs, which can cause damage to flowers and foliage. ✿ **PROPAGATION** From seed sown either in spring in cool climates or in autumn in warmer regions.

Tropaeolum majus

Nasturtium ○ ◐

✿ **OTHER NAMES** Common nasturtium, garden nasturtium
✿ **DESCRIPTION** The nasturtium is a fast-growing annual that looks very pretty in a window box, pot, or hanging basket with its foliage trailing over the sides. New varieties are compact in shape, reaching 10 inches (25 cm) in height with a spread of 10 to 18 inches (25 to 45 cm). The fragrant flowers come in bright shades of yellow, orange, and red, and the rounded leaves make a crispy addition to salads. Climbing varieties will take advantage of nearby structures and plants for support or will happily cascade over walls and banks. ✿ **PLANTING** Nasturtiums grow easily from seed sown during early spring. The potting mix should preferably be sandy or well-drained, as fertile soil will produce lush growth at the expense of the flowers. Choose a sunny position for best results and sow the seed at 1 foot (30 cm) intervals. ✿ **FLOWERING** Flowers from summer through to autumn. ✿ **CULTIVATION** Keep nasturtiums on the dry side. New growth can be trimmed at any time if it threatens to take over, and the seeds can be easily collected after flowering. Aphids and caterpillars are the main pests of the nasturtium. ✿ **PROPAGATION** By seed in spring.

INDEX OF BOTANICAL NAMES

INDEX OF COMMON NAMES

PHOTOGRAPHY CREDITS

Australian Picture Library: p. 48; **Clive Nichols:** p. 63; **Garden Picture Library**: Brian Carter p. 69, Brian Carter p. 99, Brian Carter p. 104, Christopher Fairweather p. 90, Clive Nichols p. 87, Clive Nichols p. 101, Constance Elliott p. 51, David Askam p. 43, David Russell p. 34, David Russell p. 35, Didier Willery p. 14, Didier Willery p. 105, Elizabeth Crowe p. 79, J.S. Sira p. 68, Joanne Pavia p. 83, John Glover, p. 10, John Glover p. 11, John Glover p. 16, John Glover p. 56, John Glover p. 72, Juliet Wade p. 65, Lamontagne p. 57, Lamontagne p. 67, Lamontagne p. 86, Linda Burgess p. 44, Linda Burgess p. 58, Linda Burgess p. 89, Micheal Howes p. 2, Michael Howes p. 71, Paul Windsor p. 60; **Ivy Hansen:** p. 12, p. 15, p. 19, p. 21, p. 22, p. 26, p. 28, p. 30, p. 32, p. 33, p. 42 p. 45, p. 46, p. 49, p. 52, p. 55, p. 59, p. 61, p. 64, p. 77, p. 78, p. 80, p. 81, p. 82, p. 84, p. 85, p. 91, p. 92, p. 95, p. 96,p. 97, p. 98, p. 100, p. 103, p. 107, p. 108, p. 109; **Lorna Rose:** p. 13, p. 17, p. 47, p. 50, p. 54, p. 66, p. 75, p. 88, p. 93; **Photo I Nats:** David M. Stone p. 73, Peter Margosian p. 20; **S&O Mathews:** p. 23, p. 25, p. 27, p. 29, p. 41, p. 62, p. 70, p. 74, p. 76, p. 102, p. 106; **Ward Lock:** front cover; **Lansdowne Publishing:** p. 31, p. 36, p. 37, p. 38 p. 39, p. 40, Colin Beard p. 18, Peter Shore p. 94, Tony Rodd p. 53